THE
SANDRA BULLOCK
FILES

FROM SPEED TO GRAVITY

BRIAN ROWE

First Paperback Edition: April 2014

The Sandra Bullock Files: From Speed to Gravity is a work of film criticism. At times Brian has pulled information from the Internet Movie Database, Wikipedia, Youtube videos, and DVD behind-the-scenes documentaries and audio commentaries. Other information was obtained in person at the Santa Barbara International Film Festival in February 2010. No books by other authors have been quoted in this work.

Articles on the following films, mini-series, and/or TV shows were previously published in different versions on Suite 101: *Hangmen, The Bionic Showdown, Who Shot Patakango, The Preppie Murder, Religion Inc, Working Girl, Lucky Chances, Love Potion No. 9, Me & the Mob, The Vanishing, When the Party's Over, The Thing Called Love, Fire on the Amazon, Demolition Man, Wrestling Ernest Hemingway, Speed, While You Were Sleeping, The Net, Two if by Sea, A Time to Kill, In Love & War, Speed 2: Cruise Control, Making Sandwiches, Hope Floats, Practical Magic, The Prince of Egypt, Forces of Nature, Gun Shy, 28 Days, Miss Congeniality, George Lopez, Murder by Numbers,* and *Divine Secrets of the Ya-Ya Sisterhood.* These articles have since been revised and expanded on. Brian has retained all ownership of this content.

The Sandra Bullock Files: From Speed to Gravity
ISBN-13: 978-1497419834
ISBN-10: 1497419832

For Sandra

INTRODUCTION

Why Sandra Bullock?

The star of *Speed*, *While You Were Sleeping*, *The Proposal*, and *The Heat* has been entertaining audiences the world over for nearly thirty years in both film and television. She is one of the most down-to-earth movie stars we have, one who never allows any kind of ego to outweigh the love she has for her fans. She is also an actress who seems to get better with age. Stuck as a romantic comedy queen in the early stages of her career, she has broken out as an acclaimed dramatic actress in recent years, with her memorable turns in *Crash*, *The Blind Side*, and *Gravity*.

She is one of the few actors in Hollywood who currently juggles different genres, like comedy, drama, thrillers, and science fiction, and does it successfully. Four of her six most recent films (*The Proposal*, *The Blind Side*, *The Heat*, and *Gravity*) have together accumulated more than $1.5 billion dollars at the worldwide box office. She won an Academy Award for *The Blind Side*, and was nominated again for *Gravity*. She's one of the only true movie stars we have. How is it that no one has ever written a significant book about her career until now?

1

I have been one of Sandra's biggest fans for twenty years and counting. When I was nine years old, I watched *Speed* for the first time and fell madly in love with that perky brunette behind the wheel. All these years I have followed her career, showing up for her movies, including the ones that scored with audiences, as well as the ones that didn't. And no matter if she appeared in a great film, or a horrid stinker, my love for Sandra never faltered. So what a thrill it was, after all this time, to see her appear in the film of her career—Alfonso Cuaron's remarkable *Gravity*.

In 2006 I got my first glimpse of Sandra, in Los Angeles at the premiere of *The Lake House*. *Speed* is one of my favorite movies, and it was a thrill when Sandra and Keanu Reeves both signed my two-disc DVD. That next year I made a comedy short film about a young man trying to overcome his Sandra addiction, called, appropriately, *Addiction Control*. Starring Ryan Mitchell and Scott Gairdner, the film is most definitely autobiographical.

In February of 2010, the dream finally came true, when I met Sandra at the Santa Barbara International Film Festival, where she received the Riviera Award. I told her how much I loved her and her many movies, which she responded to by saying, "Have you *seen* all my movies?" I took two pictures with her, and got to watch a great sit-down interview she had with the film critic Pete Hammond inside the auditorium. A month later, I had my fifteen minutes of Internet fame. When Sandra was nominated for her first Oscar for *The Blind Side*, I told my friends I was going to freak out if she won—so they filmed my reaction. Well, I did freak out. A little too much. The video of me screaming at the top of my lungs hit almost 100,000 hits on Youtube in a matter of hours, and Inside Edition interviewed me for their program later that week.

So, as you can see, I love Sandra Bullock. And in June of 2010 I began a four-year-long project that I feel is long overdue: the first significant book ever written about Sandra's extraordinary career. 2014 was a big year for Sandra. She was nominated for her second Oscar, for her career-best performance in *Gravity*. 2014 (June 10, exactly) marked the twentieth anniversary of her breakthrough action movie, *Speed*. And in July, the unthinkable happened: the forever youthful Sandra celebrated her fiftieth birthday. She's one of the biggest movie stars in the world, one who deserves a book about her varied and fascinating career.

The Sandra Bullock Files: From Speed to Gravity features reviews of Sandra's films, and even some of her TV show appearances. I look at her hit films, like *Speed*, *While You Were Sleeping*, *The Proposal*, and *The Blind Side*. I discuss her underrated and lesser-seen work, like *Wrestling Ernest Hemingway* and *Infamous*. I go into the movies she made early in her career, which includes many films you've probably never heard of, like *The Preppie Murder* and *Religion, Inc.* I also—I'm sorry to say—discuss her stinkers, too, like *All About Steve*, which won her a Razzie award for Worst Actress the night before she won her Oscar, and the notorious *Speed 2: Cruise Control*. Almost every film and TV project Sandra has appeared in is included here. Each review includes my analysis of the film and her performance, as well as where the film fits into her career. You will also find essential film facts (distributor, production company, release date, director, writer(s), producer(s), other significant cast members), my picks for my favorite lines and scenes from each film, and various trivia and fun facts.

Not *all* projects Sandra has been affiliated with are covered. While it was not possible to screen all twelve episodes of her 1990 TV show *Working Girl*, the show as a whole is discussed, and while the short film she wrote and directed called *Making Sandwiches* has never been released to the public, a chapter about this mysterious hidden film has been included. Not included are reviews of films she appeared as herself in (*Welcome to Hollywood*, *Lisa Picard is Famous*) or reviews of films she produced but didn't star in (*Our Father*, *Sudbury*). This is also not a book that focuses on her personal life. While I bring in some elements of Sandra's life into my analysis occasionally (in the first chapter, for example), there is no discussion in this book about her various romances, her ex-husband Jesse James, her precious son Louie. I have elected to concentrate on the work itself.

The films are discussed in order, from *Hangmen*, her film debut, all the way to *Gravity*, her greatest achievement. Are you ready to take the journey?

HANGMEN
(1987)

FILM FACTS

PRODUCTION COMPANY: Cinema Sciences Corporation
RELEASE DATE: November 1987 (Video Premiere)

DIRECTOR: J. Christian Ingvordsen
WRITERS: J. Christian Ingvordsen, Steven Kaman, Rick Washburn
(additional dialogue)
PRODUCERS: J. Christian Ingvordsen, Steven W. Kaman, Richard R.
Washburn
ALSO STARRING: Rick Washburn, Keith Bogart, J. Christian
Ingvordsen, Jake LaMotta

REVIEW

It all started with a little B-movie called *Hangmen*. But
first… let's go back.

Sandra Bullock was born in Arlington, Virginia, on July
26, 1964, to Helga Meyer, a German opera singer; and John
Bullock, a voice coach. Sandra lived in Germany in her
younger years and has remained fluent in German
throughout her adult life. Sandra has one sister named
Gesine, and the two both became heavily influenced by the

arts at a young age, Sandra studied ballet and vocal arts as a child.

In high school she started acting in local theater productions, and she was also a cheerleader. She graduated in 1982 and attended East Carolina University in North Carolina for the next four years but left prematurely in 1986, just three credits shy of graduating, to pursue an acting career. She made her way to New York to pursue auditions, and she supported herself through a variety of jobs, like cocktail waitressing.

In New York she became serious about acting and started taking acting classes at the Neighborhood Playhouse. While taking odd jobs, attending class, and going out on auditions, she finally landed her first film role. The movie is called *Hangmen*, and it is by far one of the most forgettable titles on Sandra's resume.

Before *Demolition Man* in 1993, Sandra appeared in a lot of random movies, most of which were never released to theaters or made much of an impression on anyone. There can't be a lot of people out there who genuinely love *When the Party's Over*, *The Preppie Murder*, or *Religion, Inc.* 1993 was the year she started appearing in more substantial films, but before then, the woman needed to pay her dues, as well as her bills.

Directed and co-written by some guy named J. Christian Ingvordsen, *Hangmen* is awful, so truly bad it is hard to imagine anyone involved with the production thinking their time and hard work would translate into a good movie. Sandra's first scene takes place four and a half minutes in. She sits at the foot of a statue in the middle of a

New Your City park and kisses her boyfriend rather nonchalantly. She looks almost the same in 1987 as she does now, sporting that trademark long black hair and adorable smile. Her first words ever in a movie? "Spoo head!" Her first conflict ever? "I have two tests tomorrow that I haven't even bothered to study for." Not exactly deep, but it's a start.

She isn't the main character in this mess. The plot has something to do with Danny Greene (Keith Bogart), the sixteen-year-old boyfriend to Sandra's character Lisa Edwards, discovering inside information about the CIA and having to run for his life. The music is cheesy, the cinematography is clumsy and dark, and most of the actors look like they're reading off cue cards.

The film is important for only one thing: it started Sandra's career. It's a lot of fun to watch her scenes in this, as brief and fleeting as they may be. At one point Sandra appears out of nowhere brushing her teeth, wearing only a towel. This scene, with all its funny phone props and old-school computers, brings to mind some of the absurdities of *The Net,* a thriller she would make in 1995.

About halfway through the movie, she sits and cries with concern over the disappearance of her boyfriend, Danny. It is here that we first witness Sandra's crying face, the one seen in all its glory at the end of such films as *Speed* and *Miss Congeniality.*

But the main highlight of *Hangmen* occurs at the forty-six minute mark, where, while walking outside and holding a newspaper, Sandra's character gets shot in the neck with a tranquilizer. It is as hilarious a moment that she's ever appeared in. The way she starts weaving side to side, drifting in and out of consciousness, is completely ridiculous, and has to be seen to be believed.

In the end, Sandra starts getting in on some of the action in, again, scenes in an abandoned factory that bring to mind the conclusion of *The Net*. *Hangmen* is a very bad movie, one that now only makes its way into DVD dollar bins due to Sandra's name value. If Sandra ever does *Inside the Actor's Studio* with James Lipton, it's unlikely they'll be bringing up this one.

Check out clips of *Hangmen* on Youtube for some giggles; otherwise, skip it.

BEST SCENE
Tranquilizer dart to the neck.

BEST LINE
"Why don't you come over and see me some time, big boy."

FUN FACTS

Sandra's film debut.

Despite her small role in the film, she was later featured prominently on most DVD covers.

The director went on to make more than twenty direct-to-video action movies.

THE BIONIC SHOWDOWN:
THE SIX MILLION DOLLAR MAN AND THE BIONIC WOMAN
(1989)

FILM FACTS

DISTRIBUTOR: NBC
PRODUCTION COMPANY: Michael Sloan Productions
RELEASE DATE: April 30, 1989 (TV Premiere)

DIRECTOR: Alan J. Levi
WRITERS: Michael Sloan, Brock Choy (teleplay); Michael Sloan, Robert De Laurentiis (story)
PRODUCERS: Bernadette Joyce, Nigel Watts, Richard Anderson, Lee Majors
ALSO STARRING: Lindsay Wagner, Lee Majors, Richard Anderson, Jeff Yagher

REVIEW

1987's *Hangmen*, Sandra's film debut, didn't exactly skyrocket the young actress's career to new heights, but 1989 proved to be one of her most prolific years. Sandra appeared in two feature films—*Religion, Inc* and *Who Shot Patakango?*—and two TV movies—*The Preppie Murder* and

Bionic Showdown. She even made a guest appearance on a TV show called *Starting From Scratch*.

While none of these films or roles can be looked at today as in any way memorable, these first few gigs helped get the career steamroller going for the actress, who would soon obtain her first substantial gig the following year on a TV show based on one of the most acclaimed films of 1988.

In 1973 *The Six Million Dollar Man* started a series of goofy TV movies starring Lee Majors as a test pilot who dies in a horrific crash but is brought back to life and rebuilt and equipped with nuclear powered bionic limbs and implants. The story is pretty ridiculous, but the film proved successful and ended up spawning nine sequels, as well as two TV series. Directed by Alan J. Levi, *The Bionic Showdown* was the second to last TV movie installment, with the Bionic Woman and Six Million Dollar Man re-uniting to catch a bionic spy with the help of a younger assistant.

Sandra plays that younger assistant, named Kate Mason, and she first appears in the movie about thirteen minutes in falling off a wheelchair and getting showered with gifts. It turns out her character is watching this old footage of herself on a TV screen, and she's awaiting her transformation from a woman confined to a wheelchair to becoming bionic. After a successful operation, she not only can walk but also can run faster than the *Looney Tunes* Road Runner.

While her screen time was limited in *Hangmen*, Sandra actually has a lot to do in this movie. Whenever she's not on screen, the movie is pretty standard and dull, despite some unintentionally hilarious bits where the two leads magically jump over walls. Her scenes, despite some mediocre writing, bring some life to the proceedings.

The first half of the movie features Sandra in pedestrian talky scenes that ramble, but the second half shows her having fun taking control of her bionic powers and running at the speed of light. One absurdly entertaining scene has Kate fighting off half a dozen thugs by shoving them all into bushes and trees. But no doubt her finest moment comes at the climax when Kate wards off the bad guy by jumping a hundred feet in the air, tossing a heavy ball at his groin, and kicking him into a fence that electrocutes him. Excellent work, Sandy.

While this film won't go down as one of her better efforts, there's a charm to Sandra's screen persona that can already be felt here, particularly in her romantic scenes toward the end of the movie. Her trademark smile is seen throughout, as well as blink-and-you'll-miss classic Sandra moments, like the way she says "OK" to a love interest and the smirk she flashes a competitor in the final showdown. There is also a lot of Sandra jogging in tight, multi-colored fitness clothes. My, how that girl can run.

BEST SCENE
Leaping into the air and fighting the bad guy.

BEST LINE
"That's what life is to you! JOKES!"

FUN FACTS

This was apparently a pilot for a never-produced spin-off series featuring Sandra.

Although many episodes of *The Six Million Dollar Man* and *The Bionic Woman* took place in exotic countries, this is the only episode that was actually filmed outside the United States. It was filmed in Toronto.

Lee Majors reprised his role of Steve Austin in one more *Bionic* movie called, appropriately, *Bionic Ever After?* But he also played Steve again much later, in a 2009 episode of Comedy Central's *Robot Chicken*.

WHO SHOT PATAKANGO? (1989)

FILM FACTS

PRODUCTION COMPANY: CineVu, Inc
RELEASE DATE: August 1989

DIRECTOR: Robert Brooks
WRITERS: Halle Brooks, Robert Brooks
PRODUCER: Halle Brooks
ALSO STARRING: David Edwin Knight, Kevin Otto, Chris Cardona,
Michael Puzzo

REVIEW

Sandra isn't really known for period dramas, aside from the panned *In Love and War* and the underrated *Infamous*. She has always had more success playing modern characters in a modern world. Early in her career, however, she appeared in another period film, one that is easily among her lesser known works. The movie has no external reviews to be found on the Internet Movie Database, and, aside from Allison Janney, who appears in a cameo role, nobody affiliated with the film besides Sandra went to do any notable work. This film is a curio, one only worth checking out for the absolute Sandra die-hards.

1989 was a busy year for Sandra. Casting directors were clearly starting to pick up on her wit, charm, and vulnerability, giving her opportunities in smaller films that might lead to something more substantial. The awkwardly titled *Who Shot Patakango?* (also known as *Who Shot Pat?* in many video releases) is one of those films she did in the hopes that it could lead to better projects.

The movie is pedestrian in every way, shot pretty flat and acted with banality. Unlike *Bionic Showdown*, Sandra isn't in a lot of this movie, appearing only for about twenty minutes of the running time. The first time we see her she is out in the cold at night, standing with friends. She looks utterly adorable in her period wardrobe, and she is one of the few actors in the film who brings a trace of life to the proceedings.

The film, set in Brooklyn, New York, follows a group of young teenagers in the late 1950s, with the main character Bic falling in love with Devlin (played by Sandra). He's poor, and she comes from a rich family, but *Romeo & Juliet* this isn't. Imagine *West Side Story* re-envisioned by college students flexing their filmmaking chops by making a period film for their senior thesis.

There are a few cute moments. Devlin stops a knife-fight, only to have her beau get cut in the process. Of course she has to take him back to her place to clean him up, and of course he has to take his shirt off, revealing a stunning six-pack that awkwardly doesn't make any impression on her. Later on there is foreplay on a bed between Bic and Devlin that may or may not lead to love-making; it is never clear if the two actually consummate the act.

Who Shot Patakango? is interesting only for those who want to see Sandra in an early period role, one in which she looks more youthful and gorgeous than ever. She's not given much to do here, but, in retrospect, her career had only just begun.

BEST SCENE
Sandra playing with her boyfriend on the bed.

BEST LINE
"Why… why… why… WHY!"

FUN FACTS

Who Shot Patakango? was Robert Brooks' directorial debut, writing debut, and editing debut. He never made another movie.

Allison Janney plays Miss Penny. This film marked her acting debut.

Most DVDs feature Sandra's face on the cover, but only some are pictures of her from this actual movie.

THE PREPPIE
MURDER
(1989)

FILM FACTS

DISTRIBUTOR: ABC
PRODUCTION COMPANY: Jack Grossbart Productions
RELEASE DATE: September 24, 1989 (TV Premiere)

DIRECTOR: John Herzfeld
WRITERS: John Herzfeld, Irv Roud (teleplay); Irv Roud (story)
PRODUCERS: Sydell Albert, Paul Pompian
ALSO STARRING: Danny Aiello, William Baldwin, Lara Flynn Boyle,
William Devane

REVIEW

Not every actress can get the start of someone like
Meryl Streep. Her first film co-starred Jane Fonda, her
second film co-starred Robert De Niro, and her third film
co-starred Woody Allen. In just two years she had earned
an Oscar nomination, followed by an Oscar win, for *Kramer
Vs. Kramer*. By Streep's fifth film, her gold star status was
sealed, and she would go on to enjoy one of the finest,
most respected careers in Hollywood.

It didn't really go that way for Sandra. It took her a good seven years and a long series of forgettable clunkers to really start paving the way for a big career. When Streep was twenty-eight years old, she was filming *The Deer Hunter*. When Sandra was twenty-eight, she was filming a porno! But more on that one later...

While Sandra had pretty big roles in *Bionic Woman* and *Who Shot Patakango?*, she only appears in a few minutes of the TV movie, *The Preppie Murder*, which stars William Baldwin, Danny Aiello, and Lara Flynn Boyle, and tells the true story of a murder committed by Robert Chambers, a serial killer who plead guilty to manslaughter in the death of an eighteen-year-old girl.

Sandra makes a brief appearance in this one, her hair in a ponytail, her school vest making her appear younger than she was at the time. Her character of Stacy is a throwaway part, one she probably shot in a day or two. Not that it would have been worth Sandra's time to be in more of this one; the TV movie was not well received. Debuting on ABC, and directed by John Herzfeld, *The Preppie Murder* is, unfortunately, another clunker in Sandra's early career. In fact, she's given so little to do here that there is no **Best Scene** or **Best Line** this time around.

FUN FACTS

This film helped launch the careers of not just Sandra, but also William Baldwin, Lara Flynn Boyle, and Diedrich Bader, the latter of whom would go on to co-star with Sandra in *Miss Congeniality 2: Armed and Fabuous*.

—

The lead detective in the real case, Mike Sheehan, makes a cameo appearance.

Chris Isaak provided the music for the soundtrack.

RELIGION, INC. (1989)

FILM FACTS

DISTRIBUTOR: Trinity Home Entertainment
PRODUCTION COMPANY: Blossom Pictures
RELEASE DATE: September 1989

DIRECTOR: Daniel Adams
WRITERS: Michael Mailer; Daniel Adams (story)
PRODUCERS: Sydell Albert, Paul Pompian
ALSO STARRING: Jonathan Penner, George Plimpton, Gerald Orange, Wendy Adams

REVIEW

The lackluster comedy *Religion, Inc*, tells of a New York adman who forms a new religion based on greed, with Sandra playing the role of his skeptical girlfriend. She first appears about six minutes into the movie, finding her boyfriend shirtless and drunk. Why is it that every movie Sandra made in the 1980s is so technically inadequate, not just with the cinematography, but with the sound quality as well? And what's with the misplaced country music soundtrack? Here's another early Sandra movie clearly made my people who don't understand the most rudimentary factors of filmmaking.

Sandra plays a lawyer here—it's a precursor to *A Time To Kill!*—named Debby Cosgrove, but unfortunately she has very little to do in this movie. She shows up in a random scene every twenty minutes or so, usually upset with her boyfriend's get-rich-quick scheme. Her only notable scene comes toward the end, when she counsels an African-American man, impressing him with her striking gray business suit. Just look at her in this scene—she looks the same here as she does today!

Nothing Sandra made in 1989 is worth seeking out, except for the die-hard fans. The only joy one can have in watching these movies is to see Sandra trying to make the most of mediocre parts, long before she had the power to choose roles on her own. The only film released that year that offers any entertainment value is *Bionic Woman*; if you were going to watch one of her '80s movies, that would be your best choice.

BEST SCENE
Sandra tries to counsel a jive-talking African-American man.

BEST LINE
"The point is, can we prove that you're not a pimp?"

FUN FACTS

Also known as *A Fool and His Money*.

———

Despite the film's low reputation, the director Daniel Adams went on to direct many more films, including a 2009 period movie called *The Lightkeepers*, starring Academy Award winner Richard Dreyfuss.

WORKING GIRL (1990)

TV SHOW FACTS

DISTRIBUTOR: NBC
PRODUCTION COMPANY: 20th Century Fox Entertainment
PREMIERE DATE: April 16, 1990

DIRECTOR: Matthew Diamonds (5 episodes)
WRITER: Robin Schiff (4 episodes)
PRODUCERS: Stephanie Hagen; Matthew Diamond (consulting)
ALSO STARRING: George Newbern, Anthony Tyler Quinn, Judy Prescott, Tom O'Rourke

REVIEW

By the turn of the new decade, Sandra had starred in a handful of films but had made hardly a blip on Hollywood's radar. She needed something more mainstream, more highly publicized, to get her to the next step in her career. Finally, in 1990, Sandra took advantage of a great opportunity and never looked back.

The Mike Nichols directed film *Working Girl* was one of the big hits of 1988. It starred Harrison Ford, Sigourney Weaver, Alec Baldwin, Joan Cusack, and Oliver Platt, and it gave newcomer Melanie Griffith the best role of her career. It won an Academy Award and was nominated for five more. Clearly this film was a success, and two years later, many involved decided to go ahead not with a sequel, but with a TV sitcom. Of course nobody from the original movie would head over to the show—Ford probably had better things to do—and an entirely new cast was brought on board.

Who did the producers turn to in late 1989 before filming was to commence? They didn't want a nobody. They wanted a familiar TV face. So they cast *The Facts of Life*'s Nancy McKeon, in the lead role of Tess McGill, a secretary who becomes a junior executive of her company. With a long list of credits dating back fifteen years, McKeon seemed a decent enough choice for the role. But when she dropped out, Sandra took a chance, auditioned, and nabbed the role just weeks before shooting commenced.

Created by Kimberly Hill and Tom Patchett, the series premiered on NBC on April 16, 1990, with an episode called "Dream On." A mid-season replacement, *Working Girl* didn't go too far. The network only aired nine of its initial twelve episodes and canned the show soon thereafter.

The show intro promises great cheesiness to come. Sandra walks around New York with her big early '90s frizzy hair, smiling as if she can hear that annoying (Oscar-winning!) background music in her head. She has been known to say that working on this show was one of the worst professional acting experiences of her life. Unfortunately these twelve episodes are not available to watch, but of the few clips available it's pretty clear why she felt that way.

The best thing that came out of this show was more exposure for Sandra, who finally had a major credit on her resume to get her to her next job. While her truly big break wouldn't be for another four years, the *Working Girl* TV series allowed her to test her skills in a new format—multi-camera television—and make her decide, thankfully, to pursue film instead.

BEST SCENE
That classic '90s intro.

BEST LINE
"Me. Tess McGill from Stanton Island!"

FUN FACTS

Working Girl marked Sandra's only starring role on a TV show.

Episode titles include "I Heard It Through the Grapevine," "Hungry Heart," and "Guess Who's Coming to Dinner," the latter of which was the last episode aired, on July 30, 1990.

The four episodes never aired are titled "Get Back," "Two's a Crowd," "We Can Work It Out," and "Oh, Brother."

—

The series briefly reran on TV Land in the 1990s after Sandra became a major star.

Working Girl has never been released to DVD.

LUCKY CHANCES (1990)

MINISERIES FACTS

DISTRIBUTOR: NBC
PREMIERE DATE: October 7, 1990

DIRECTOR: Buzz Kulik
WRITER: Jackie Collins (based on her books *Chances* and *Lucky*)
PRODUCER: William Peters
ALSO STARRING: Vincent Irizarry, Eric Braeden, Elizabeth Moss, Nicolette Sheridan

REVIEW

By 1990, Sandra was slowly appearing in more and more projects that would eventually lead to more legitimate opportunities. But until 1992, when she got her first big screen leading role, she found herself stuck in mediocre movies and television programs. In 1990 after she shot twelve episodes of her failed NBC show *Working Girl*, she appeared in *Lucky Chances*, based on the novels *Chances* and *Lucky* by Jackie Collins.

The four-and-a-half-hour mini-series, which aired on NBC in October 1990 and later won an Emmy Award for Outstanding Cinematography, tells of the rise of a powerful man in the Las Vegas casino industry and his daughter's struggle to maintain the family empire. Sandra plays the supporting role of Maria Santangelo, who unfortunately gets killed off at the end of Part 1.

Like most everything Sandra made up until 1993, *Lucky Chances* is a dreary, talky mess. It is acted poorly, shot amateurishly, and moves way too slowly. Worse, it takes forty-five minutes for Sandra to even appear. She does get an entrance though, stumbling into a kitchen with a loving musical score accompanying her.

Sandra is stunning in this, maybe more so than in any of her early work. She's got a glow about her, as if she's finally starting to relax into her profession. (Or maybe she was happy to be out of sitcom Hell.) She gets to wear pretty black dresses, let her hair down all long and glamarous, and smile in almost every scene. She doesn't have a whole lot to do in this—she mostly looks lovingly at her husband while playing with their children and throwing birthday parties—but she looks fantastic.

The only real scene of note is Maria's unexpected demise. How many movies have Sandra died in? Not many. (She is killed off pretty early in *The Vanishing*, but off-screen.) She's throwing a birthday party and is approached by a strange-looking man who inquires about her husband's whereabouts. A few scenes later, her character's daughter discovers her floating dead in a pool, blood dripping from her mouth. This might be the only time in Sandra's career she ever played a corpse!

Lucky Chances is important in Sandra's resume for two reasons. One, it was the first and only time she appeared in a TV mini-series. And two, it was her last major television appearance (outside of an episode of *Muppets Tonight* and some guest appearances on *The George Lopez Show*). After this, it would be nothing but feature films.

BEST SCENE
Sandra's death scene – lying on a raft in the pool.

BEST LINE
"Hey, big boy, you wanna stay here and play?"

FUN FACTS

At 272 minutes, this is the longest project Sandra has ever appeared in.

This mini-series was followed by a sequel called *Lady Boss*, which premiered in 1992.

Elizabeth Moss, who would go on to great accolades in *Mad Men* and *Top of the Lake*, plays six-year-old Lucky.

LOVE POTION NO. 9 (1992)

FILM FACTS

DISTRIBUTOR: 20th Century Fox
PRODUCTION COMPANY: Penta Pictures
RELEASE DATE: November 13, 1992

DIRECTOR: Dale Launer
WRITER: Dale Launer
PRODUCER: Dale Launer
ALSO STARRING: Tate Donovan, Mary Mara, Anne Bancroft, Dylan
Baker

REVIEW

Well here it is, Sandra's first starring role in a movie
that marked both a big break as well as a potential career
ender all at the same time. Before *Love Potion No. 9*,
Sandra's performances in movies were relegated to
insignificant supporting roles that typically didn't amount to
much. Furthermore, the movies themselves were tiny
productions that never reached a wide audience. *Love Potion
No. 9* was not only her first major film role, but also her
first major studio movie. She's the female lead here, and it's
a great pleasure to watch her finally take a big bite into a

juicy role. But the film's abysmal failure at the box office almost resulted in Sandra's career coming to an abrupt end.

The movie is pretty dumb and goofy—there's no sign of an Oscar yet in Sandra's future here. But this movie marks the first performance of her career where she gets to finally create a character, one with goals and flaws and charm. She has a full arc over the course of the movie and gets the chance to show off her comedic skills, as well as her early, underdeveloped dramatic ones. She also becomes gradually prettier as the movie goes on, allowing us to see all the sides of 1992 Sandra in their full glory. In fact the ugly-duckling-turned-swan scenario in this film is reminiscent of one of her most successful comedies—*Miss Congeniality*.

When we're first introduced to her, she looks comically ridiculous. She's got thick glasses, buck teeth, a dopey wardrobe, and stringy hair falling into places it shouldn't. Sandra plays Diane, a shy biochemist who's never had any luck with men, until one day her good friend Paul (the only guy she's ever had a date with), played by Tate Donovan, gives her a potion he received from a gypsy (Anne Bancroft). She tries the elixir scientifically at first, to see if she can get out of a traffic ticket. But before she realizes the true power of the potion, she finds herself on the other side of the magic, when a total slime-ball uses it to get her to marry him. The second half of the film is frustrating, to say the least, as Diane remains under the man's spell, and the audience knows full well that Paul is the one she should be with.

30

The movie opened in wide release in November 1992 and was poised to become a potential hit comedy. Instead, it completely tanked, taking in only three quarters of a million dollars at the domestic box office. The career of writer and first-time director Dale Launer never recovered and Donovan, who went on to date Sandra for much of the early '90s, never made it to the A-list (although he has gone on to a busy career directing television).

After this movie tanked, Sandra found herself back at square one. When her name was tossed around as an idea for the role of Annie in *Speed*, Fox executives wouldn't have it—to them, the box office failure of *Love Potion No. 9* was in part due to Sandra's non-existent star power. The casting Gods had their way, however, and she nabbed the role that would finally catapult her to superstardom.

Of course, upon the release of *Love Potion No. 9*, summer 1994 was still many months away. Sandra had a few more films to make, some good, some bad, and one so disastrous it too could have put a stop to her career.

BEST SCENE
Her first scene where she, looking her worst, explains to a group of attractive women the important biological work she does with chimpanzees.

BEST LINE
"I'm a comparative psycho biologist!"

—

FUN FACTS

Also known as *Love Potion #9*.

Inspired by the 1959 song written by Jerry Leiber and Mike Stoller.

This film grossed $754,935 at the box office.

Despite her prominence on the DVD cover, Sandra wasn't even featured on the original poster.

ME & THE MOB
(1992)

FILM FACTS

DISTRIBUTOR: Santelmo Entertainment
PRODUCTION COMPANY: RSVP Productions
RELEASE DATE: 1992

DIRECTOR: Frank Rainone
WRITERS: James Lorinz, Frank Rainone, Rocco Simonelli
PRODUCERS: Frank Rainone, Vincent Viola
ALSO STARRING: James Lorinz, Tony Darrow, Vincent Pastore,
Steve Buscemi

REVIEW

Before we get to the very busy year for Sandra that was 1993, we need to take a look at the last of her little-seen, barely released work. She only has two scenes in the reprehensible *Me and the Mob*, but one is definitely memorable.

Directed by Frank Rainone, this film sat on the shelf for a couple of years and didn't get a proper release until Sandra's star power started to climb. It tells of a struggling writer who takes a job with the mob to pay the rent, and the film stars James Lorinz in the lead role, as well as *The*

Sopranos' Vinny Pastore and Steve Buscemi in supporting roles.

Sandra's first scene stands out the most and marks one of her most bizarre on-screen moments. She shows up at the writer's apartment, proceeds to strip to her black bra and undies, and then simulates sex on top of him while he asks her questions about what makes great writing. All of this plays out in one single shot. Sandra commits to the best of her ability, but it's difficult to understand why she ever agreed to appear in this amateurish movie. Maybe she was a few months behind on rent payments?

BEST SCENE
Sandra's over-the-top sex scene on an office chair.

BEST LINE
"Writing is about living, okay? Writing is the least of it!"

FUN FACTS

Also known as *Who Do I Gotta Kill?*

This film was quietly released in 1992 but got a big push on video in late 1994 after Sandra became famous.

THE VANISHING (1993)

FILM FACTS

DISTRIBUTOR: 20th Century Fox
RELEASE DATE: February 5, 1993

DIRECTOR: George Sluizer
WRITER: Todd Graff (based on the novel by Tim Krabbe)
PRODUCERS: Larry Brezner, Paul Schiff, Todd Graff
ALSO STARRING: Jeff Bridges, Kiefer Sutherland, Nancy Travis, Park Overall

REVIEW

It's a third-rate version of the far more effective and chilling 1988 original, and she's only in a handful of scenes, but this 1993 version of *The Vanishing*, directed by the same guy who made the first one (George Sluizer), was probably the most important movie Sandra appeared in at this point in her career. You see, the casting director for *The Vanishing* was Risa Bramon Garcia, who would go on to cast a little movie called *Speed*. Does Sandra have Garcia to thank for making her a star? There's rarely just one person who jumpstarts an actor's successful career, but thanking Garcia would probably be a good place to start.

The film opens with the villain Barney (a dopey Jeff Bridges) going through the motions of how to chloroform his first victim, which of course takes away most of the suspense of what's to come. It is always creepier what we *don't* see. What if *Psycho* opened with Norman Bates testing out different knives and wigs in his kitchen? The shower scene probably would have had about five percent of its power.

In the first scene away from Bridges, we find Sandra sitting in the passenger seat of a car, next to Kiefer Sutherland. They play Diane and Jeff, a couple who is going on what they hope to be a relaxing vacation. Unfortunately, their car breaks down in the middle of a dark tunnel and Jeff goes to get help, while Diane waits for him. In this scene Sandra showcases a pair of super short-shorts, the kind rarely seen today (but she still pulls them off nicely).

By minute seventeen, the couple is stopping at a gas station to fill up on gas and food. She makes him swear that he'll never abandon her like that again, and we see that ultra-charming Sandra we've come to know and love. In particular a happy dance jig she does on the way to the food mart may be one of her cutest moments ever caught on film.

Sandra's at her most adorable in the beginning of the movie, so of course it seems imminent that things aren't going to end well for her. She quickly disappears, and we, the audience, know why—Bridges is seen briefly in the food mart before she walks into the bathroom. The film then continues on as Sutherland does all he can to find her, to no avail. He strikes up a friendship with Rita, played by

So I Married an Axe Murderer's Nancy Travis. This section of the film is pretty bland, with an awkward romance blossoming between the two that feels far less natural than the romance that existed between Jeff and Diane. Sandra and Sutherland have more chemistry together (an element that heightened the tension between them in a much different scenario in *A Time to Kill*).

Finally, in the second half, we get a flashback to show what really happened to Diane. Barney bumps into her in front of the bathroom and starts making polite conversation with her. This scene is somewhat chilling due to the fact that we know she's about to be attacked in the parking lot, but it's also a highly memorable one because Bridges and Sandra went on seventeen years later to win Best Actor and Best Actress at the 2010 Academy Awards. Who knew they would go from a tense scene in a subpar thriller to dual wins of the highest honor at the Oscars?

After Diane is chloroformed, we never see her again, despite a disturbing moment at the end when Sutherland acknowledges her grave. We don't want to think Sandra's in there! Except for her brief turn in the TV mini-series *Lucky Chances*, this is the only film to date that Sandra's character has perished in. Let's hope it remains the last!

She's not exactly the star of *The Vanishing*, but her presence is felt throughout, particularly when she's missing for that middle lugubrious hour. The film is most notable for being her first collaboration with casting director Risa Bramon Garcia, as well as for being her biggest studio movie yet (the budget was $20 million).

And then there are those scenes with Bridges. Be sure to watch the video of Sandra accepting her Golden Globe for *The Blind Side*. Before she makes it to the main steps, Bridges stands up and gives Sandra a kiss on the cheek. Here's hoping she wasn't for a brief second expecting a napkin of chloroform.

BEST SCENE
Sandra makes awkward conversation with a creepy Jeff Bridges.

BEST LINE
When Sandra's Chloroformed: "NOOOOOOOOO!"

FUN FACTS

With a budget of $20 million, this US remake cost over ten million times what George Sluizer's original Dutch version did in 1988.

In the original version, Jeff dies at the end, and Barney survives, without getting caught.

WHEN THE PARTY'S OVER (1993)

FILM FACTS

DISTRIBUTOR: Strand Releasing
PRODUCTION COMPANY: Emby Eye
RELEASE DATE: March 12, 1993

DIRECTOR: Matthew Irmas
WRITER: Ann Wycoff
PRODUCERS: James A. Holt, Matthew Irmas, Ann Wycoff
ALSO STARRING: Rae Dawn Chong, Kris Kamm, Elizabeth
Berridge, Brian McNamara

REVIEW

This is a film that is very low on Sandra fans' radars. It is a rambling and talky indie relationship drama that features three straight women and one gay man going through life's struggles after college while living in a house together in Los Angeles. Sandra plays Amanda, and she appears in the opening scene in silhouette. Her first line in the second scene is a doozy: "Who the fuck finished off my Captain Crunch?"

She looks the same in this movie as she does today it's incredible, really, to think that more than twenty years have passed since Sandra shot this movie, and she looks today as stunning as she did then. All that's different about her appearance here is that her signature black hair is curlier than usual.

The main reason to check out this film is to see Sandra play a foul-mouthed character. She has never dropped as many f-bombs in a movie as she does here. In fact, she's never played a character this unlikable, aside from maybe the racist wife in *Crash*. Amanda can be pretty nasty to other characters at times and definitely likes to say what's on her mind. The movie itself is wandering and aimless—think a movie like *Magnolia* or *Grand Canyon*, but without a decent script. However, it's still fun to see Sandra in such a giant role, which was one of her bigger ones at the time.

BEST SCENE
Sandra playfully flirts with a guy in a bathtub.

BEST LINE
Sandra's voice-mail message: "WHHHHAAAAAAT?!?"

FUN FACTS

This is one of Sandra's few R-rated comedies.

1993 will forever be Sandra's most prolific year. Think her 2009 was busy, with three major films released? In 1993, she appeared in six.

———

THE THING CALLED LOVE (1993)

FILM FACTS

DISTRIBUTOR: Paramount Pictures
PRODUCTION COMPANY: Davis Entertainment
RELEASE DATE: July 16, 1993

DIRECTOR: Peter Bogdanovich
WRITER: Carol Heikkinen
PRODUCERS: John Davis, Darlene K. Chan
ALSO STARRING: Samantha Mathis, River Phoenix, Dermot
Mulroney, Trisha Yearwood

REVIEW

It took Sandra a few years to build some career momentum, but everything finally started going her way around this time. One of Sandra's lesser-known 1993 titles is *The Thing Called Love*, starring Samantha Mathis (who would become a best friend of Sandra's), Dermot Mulroney, Trisha Yearwood, and River Phoenix, in one of his final film roles. Directed by Peter Bogdanovich (*The Last Picture Show*), the film tells of the turbulent journey of Miranda Presley (Mathis), who develops a friendship with

Linda Lue (Sandra) and a relationship with James Wright (Phoenix) while trying to make a name for herself in the music world.

While the star of the film is Mathis, Sandra is in a large part of it, too. She shows up about eleven minutes into the movie, wearing a purple cowgirl outfit and speaking with a Tennessee twang (long before she donned that blonde hair in *The Blind Side*). She proceeds to sing a song titled "Heaven Knocking On My Door." How often does Sandra sing in movies? Not often, so this is a special, wonderfully mellow scene.

There are many cute moments of Sandra throughout this unremarkable movie, as well as one of her finest dramatic moments up until that time in her career when she lashes out at Miranda for moving out of their motel. The whole scene is played in one shot as Linda tears through a magazine in the background, her anger slowly building. She then runs up to her friend and screams at her about her actions. It's a powerhouse of a dramatic scene, the kind that doesn't appear anywhere else in the film, that shows yet another reason why Sandra suddenly found herself booking more parts at this time.

She unfortunately disappears for the final act, a blasé forty-five minutes that just go on and on—the film is two hours long and feels close to three. Once the focus veers away from Sandra's character completely, a lot of the fun drains away, and we're stuck with a main character who is just not interesting enough to sustain the length of a feature film. But Sandra escapes the movie unscathed, having delivered easily her best performance in a motion picture so far in her blossoming career, one that was mere months away from exploding.

BEST SCENE
Sandra has an emotional meltdown in a barbershop.

BEST LINE
"And who gets their hair cut by Elvis' barber, anyway!?!"

FUN FACTS

All cast members, including Sandra, performed their own songs.

Sandra co-wrote the song, "Heaven Knocking On My Door."

While she appeared in many films in 1993, only one would be a breakaway hit. Unfortunately, it wasn't this one. *The Thing Called Love* was the most financially unsuccessful film of 1993, earning only $1 million from a budget of $14 million.

FIRE ON THE AMAZON (1993)

FILM FACTS

DISTRIBUTOR: Anchor Bay Entertainment
PRODUCTION COMPANY: Concorde-New Horizons
RELEASE DATE: October 1993

DIRECTOR: Luis Llosa
WRITERS: Luana Anders, Catherine Cyran, Beverly Gray
PRODUCERS: Luis Llosa; Roger Corman (executive producer)
ALSO STARRING: Craig Sheffer, Juan Fernandez, Judith Chapman

REVIEW

Let's tell the truth: Sandra has been in some bad movies. Despite her charm and likability, Sandra for many years struggled with picking the right scripts (or, more likely, just wasn't offered good projects). Of all the movies she has made throughout her nearly thirty-year career, maybe six or seven are good, and only three or four can be considered *great*. She has appeared in many stinkers, like her first movie *Hangmen*, and the disappointing *Speed 2*, but very little she has done comes close to the atrocity of the Roger Corman produced *Fire on the Amazon*.

Shot in 1990 but not released until 1993, and looking like it was filmed with a shoddy amateur film camera from the 1970s, this movie is often considered in the Sandra canon as being her one and only "porno" flick. Really, though, the hype surrounding the sex and nudity in this movie is just that: hype. *Fire on the Amazon* is not a pornographic movie in any way, and the highly publicized scene in question only lasts a couple of minutes and is much more yawn-inducing than it is titillating. Yet the movie continues to get one DVD re-release after another, with all sorts of different photo-shopped Sandras on their covers. Most annoying of all is the film's Blu-ray cover, which prominently displays at the top: "Academy Award Winner Sandra Bullock." Oy, vey.

Sandra plays Alyssa, a rainforest preservationist who teams with a photographer (the creepy Craig Sheffer) to solve a murder by traveling to the Amazon. It tries to be a lot of things at once: an ecological-friendly drama; a passionate, steamy romance; a heart-pounding action film. And yet it fails at everything. Think *Troll 2*, but without the entertainment value. The only redeeming factor of the film is Sandra's performance, but even she appears to know she's in a bomb and doesn't really try. Of course it doesn't help that she has a lackluster and downright bizarre leading man to act alongside with.

While the sex scene halfway through the film is definitely the most interesting aspect to the whole movie, it's fascinating for all the wrong reasons. There is nothing remotely sexy about this scene. First of all, there are the awkward camera angles. Second, there's the awful, rainforest music. Third, there's the terrifying Shaffer, who licks and thrusts his way into bad sex scene history. And fourth, Sandra placed duct tape on her breasts just to be certain that the filmmakers wouldn't show any of her naughty bits. Therefore the scene is cut up into brief, awkward moments, where Sandra looks more miserable about the filming than excited about her horny acting partner. Who could blame her?

Sandra probably wants every copy of this film to be shredded, but it simply won't go away. To Sandra fans everywhere, it's considered "that sex film," and if the movie had been cheesy fun, there might have been something to appreciate here. But as it stands among Sandra's lousy early work, this is her worst effort by far. It's too bad in 1990 that this bland project came along, she said yes, she collected her paycheck, and now she has to walk into Best Buys all around the world seeing Blu-rays of *Fire on the Amazon* promoting the work of Academy Award winner Sandra Bullock. You live and learn, right?

BEST SCENE
The sex scene, for all the wrong reasons.

BEST LINE
"Write about what you feel, not about what you see, OK?!?"

FUN FACTS

Also known as *Lost Paradise*.

—

Sandra not only placed duct tape on her breasts during the sex scene; she also made the production company sign a contract stating which parts of her were not to be shown.

The director Luis Llosa went on to direct Sylvester Stallone and Sharon Stone in *The Specialist*, another film with a highly publicized sex scene.

DEMOLITION MAN (1993)

FILM FACTS

DISTRIBUTOR: Warner Bros.
PRODUCTION COMPANY: Silver Pictures
RELEASE DATE: October 8, 1993

DIRECTOR: Marco Brambilla
WRITERS: Daniel Waters, Robert Reneau, Peter M. Lenkov
PRODUCERS: Joel Silver, Howard G. Kazanjian, Michael Levy
ALSO STARRING: Sylvester Stallone, Wesley Snipes, Denis Leary,
Benjamin Bratt

REVIEW

Does Sandra have *A League of Their Own*'s Lori Petty to thank for her career? It's possible, considering Sandra replaced Petty in this 1993 action blockbuster a few days into filming. Petty broke out with films like *Point Break* and the aforementioned *League*, only to see her career stall before it even started with the Pauly Shore vehicle *In the Army Now* and her one starring role in *Tank Girl*. She could have added another major film to her list in 1993 with the Sylvester Stallone / Wesley Snipes action thriller *Demolition Man*, but when she disagreed with producer Joel Silver over the direction of her character, she was fired, giving Sandra the opportunity to join a film that would be her first of two major breaks.

In *Demolition Man*, Sandra plays Lenina Huxley, a lieutenant in 2032 Los Angeles (now called San Angeles), who happens to be fascinated with the ways of the world prior to the year 2010, when a major earthquake destroyed everything between Los Angeles and San Diego. When an evil crime lord Simon Phoenix (Snipes) breaks out of his cryogenic prison, where he's been frozen since 1996, a troubled cop John Spartan (Stallone), who was also frozen due to negligence, is released from the prison in order to take down bad guy Simon. Lenina is then put in charge to take care of John, alerting him to all the recent developments, including the new norm for sexual intercourse, updated voice activations, and the lack of toilet paper in bathroom stalls.

Before *Demolition Man*, Sandra had appeared in multiple independent films, and even had her own television show for a brief run, but nothing she had appeared in before had reached the level of audience awareness as a new science fiction blockbuster starring world-renowned movie stars like Stallone and Snipes. While she appeared in a whopping six films in 1993, this was finally the big, juicy role in a major motion picture that she needed to bring her to the forefront of casting directors' minds. While her next big picture, released in 1994, would be the definitive film to put her on the map, *Demolition Man* remains Sandra's first major step toward stardom.

But is the flick actually any good? More than two decades since its release, the movie still plays extremely well, with plenty of action, drama, romance, and a mix of intentional comedy—"he's finally matched his meat, you really licked his ass"—and unintentional comedy—the opening shot that shows the Hollywood sign on fire in the future year of… 1996! What some may have forgotten is that Sandra has very much a lead role in the film, and probably has more screen time than Snipes, who's credited on the poster above the title. And this isn't some bland female love interest role, either, with nothing for Sandra to play. She inhabits the character as if she's a naïve five-year-old child, curious about the city's history, trying to spout twentieth century action hero lines, only interested in the kind of sex with John that will prevent the sharing of fluids.

But in the end, even though Sandra has had few chances during the film's running time to show off her ass-kicking skills, she gets one great scene in which she takes down a thug in an applause-worthy manner. This is a role that easily could have been annoying with a different actress—Petty, included—but Sandra makes Lenina both endearing and believable, hard to come by in a science fiction action flick set in the far-off future.

While some might not consider *Demolition Man* among the best of Sandra's efforts, it's certainly worth watching for those who miss that special time in the mid-90s when Sandra actually made action movies! From 1993 to 1997 she made four action flicks, but the failure of *Speed 2* prevented her from ever making another one for sixteen long years.

BEST SCENE

Tie—Sandra kicking ass toward the end before Stallone knocks her unconscious, and the "sex scene" between Sandra and Stallone

BEST LINE

"You are even better live than on laserdisc!"

FUN FACTS

Demolition Man remained her only science fiction film until Alfonso Cuaron's *Gravity*.

When asked where she learned her kicks, Sandra's character Lenina answers that she learned from watching Jackie Chan movies. In 2014, upon receiving her Critic's Choice Award for Best Actress in an Action Movie for *Gravity*, she thanked Jackie Chan for everything he's taught her.

Sandra's costume during the Taco Bell sequence was made of stones and gems weighing approximately forty pounds.

Sandra would go on to co-star with Denis Leary in *Two If By Sea* and Benjamin Bratt in *Miss Congeniality*.

WRESTLING ERNEST HEMINGWAY (1993)

FILM FACTS

DISTRIBUTOR: Warner Bros.
RELEASE DATE: December 17, 1993

DIRECTOR: Randa Haines
WRITER: Steve Conrad
PRODUCERS: Todd Black, Joe Wizan, Jim Van Wyck
ALSO STARRING: Robert Duvall, Richard Harris, Shirley MacLaine,
Piper Laurie

REVIEW

Now, hear we are, at the last stop of Sandra's career before her breakthrough *Speed*, released in June 1994, catapulted her to superstardom. And what a gem this is. Unavailable on DVD until 2010, *Wrestling Ernest Hemingway* is an underrated film from 1993, directed by Randa Haines (*Children of a Lesser God*). The film tells of a tender friendship between two elderly men (Duvall and Harris), and Sandra is at her adorable best as the waitress who enjoys conversation with the eccentric Duvall. He orders six pieces of bacon with four pieces of toast every day for breakfast, and she begs him to order something healthier, but he never does, and she always gives in.

In the beginning Sandra's role as the caring, happy-go-lucky waitress seems like a throwaway character, but the role evolves over the course of the picture, with Duvall's feelings for her becoming more and more important to the character's arc by the end. At one point Elaine announces she's moving out of town, and it appears as if her character will never be seen again. But Duvall goes to visit her one last time, and a brief scene inside her home provides one of the most endearing moments of the entire movie.

Of all the films she made in 1993, Sandra must have had a special time making this one, working alongside two Hollywood legends. While the movie didn't do well at the box office (only taking in $231,000), it's worth seeking out, not just for Sandra fans, who won't be disappointed by her bigger-than-expected role here, but also for those simply looking for a great story. *Wrestling Ernest Hemingway* is a fine piece of entertainment, and the perfect segue into the next stage of Sandra's blossoming film career.

BEST SCENE
Her final scene in the film, where she talks to Duvall at her home.

BEST LINE
"You rode all the way here on *that?*"

Micole Mercurio, who plays the waitress Bernice, also co-starred with Sandra in *While You Were Sleeping* and *The Thing Called Love*.

At her last visit at *The Tonight Show with Jay Leno* in February 2014, Sandra discussed some of her older films, including *Wrestling Ernest Hemingway*. She said, "That was one of my first jobs. I had been in awe of Richard Harris and Robert Duvall… it was just unbelievable." Leno then had this to say about when he first took notice of her: "When I saw you in *Wrestling Ernest Hemingway*, I looked at you the way I looked at my wife for the first time. You just popped, and I thought, my God, this person's gotta be a big star. And it all came true."

SPEED
(1994)

FILM FACTS

DISTRIBUTOR: 20th Century Fox
RELEASE DATE: June 10, 1994

DIRECTOR: Jan de Bont
WRITER: Graham Yost
PRODUCER: Mark Gordon
ALSO STARRING: Keanu Reeves, Dennis Hopper, Jeff Daniels, Joe
Morton, Beth Grant, Alan Ruck

REVIEW

Sandra made six films in 1993 and only one in 1994.
But that lone title in 1994 was finally the one that shot her
into superstardom. *Speed*, one of the biggest blockbusters of
its year, is one of the most fast-paced, brilliantly
constructed, endlessly exciting action movies ever made.
No matter her successes in the last twenty years, including
romantic comedy hits and an Academy Award for *The Blind
Side*—Jan de Bont's *Speed*, with its smart script and
compelling characters, remains one of her two best films,
second only to *Gravity*.

Casting director Risa Bramon Garcia, who cast Sandra in *The Vanishing* and in *Speed* (and naturally can be given a lot of the credit for Sandra's career) told me at her home that Sandra wasn't the first choice for the role of Annie, and that other actresses were considered, with Halle Berry at one point being offered the role. Garcia thought Sandra was perfect for *Speed*, but the studio wasn't too keen on her. Her previous film for 20th Century Fox—*Love Potion Number 9*—had been one of the biggest bombs of 1992, and they had no interest in pursuing her for their upcoming projects. Even Sandra's agent at the time, not thrilled with the idea of his client doing another action movie right after *Demolition Man*, tried to dissuade her from auditioning. But Garcia persisted, ultimately convinced Sandra's team to let her audition—and the rest is history.

Speed was made for just $28 million, very low at the time for a studio action film, and 20th Century Fox never looked at it as one of their most promising summer movies. They intended to dump *Speed* in August, while the sure-fire action blockbuster, James Cameron's *True Lies*, would be released in July. But then something magical happened—Fox had an early preview of *Speed*. And the response was so through-the-roof that the studio decided to make an unthinkable last-minute decision to push the movie up two months to June 10. While post-production on the film was obviously hurried, the move to earlier in the summer marked one of Fox's best decisions of the '90s, as *Speed* went on to become one of the biggest hits of 1994, and one of the most beloved action movies of the last twenty years.

Why is *Speed* one of the best action movies ever made? Most of all, it has a great concept that's executed flawlessly. A lot of directors could have made a movie about a bus that can't drop below fifty miles an hour (and the studio certainly met with other possibilities, including Walter Hill, as well as someone who wanted to shoot all the bus material on a soundstage!), but Jan de Bont, a former cinematographer who shot *Die Hard* and made his directorial debut on *Speed*, proved to be the best choice for this material. Despite its complete absurdity, with one improbable action sequence after another, the viewer buys everything that happens because of the assured confidence of the top-notch directing.

And viewers don't just believe the crazy events through the movie; they, some way or another, actually care about the characters, too. Very few action movies, even the ones made by the greatest of directors, feature charming, memorable characters—the emphasis is usually always on the stunts. And if there was any film script in history to toss aside its characters for eye-popping nonstop action, *Speed* would have been it. But what makes the film endure today are the terrific performances by its ensemble cast, and the unexpected but winning romantic chemistry between Sandra and Keanu Reeves.

Reeves is at his toughest and most lovable in *Speed*, and the late Dennis Hopper, famous for playing bad guys, delivers one of his most iconic performances of his career. Jeff Daniels thought he was making a turd while shooting *Speed* and was surprised more than anyone when the movie actually turned out to be good—he has some great moments in the movie, particularly his haunting last shot. On the bus are many terrific character actors, too, including Alan Ruck and Beth Grant, who both add humor and humanity to the proceedings.

But it's Sandra's courageous and relaxed performance that brings out the best in *Speed*, playing everything as truth, displaying her winning personality even in the midst of chaos and confusion. While she had a chance in 1993's *Demolition Man* to showcase her charm, much of her performance in that action movie is her playing an ignorant goofball. In *Speed* she's an everywoman, an L.A. native forced to ride the bus to work because of her many speeding tickets, and she elects to drive the massive vehicle in a moment of panic when the driver is accidentally shot. There's nothing fake or phony about her performance. She draws you in with her smile and relatable personality, but it's her honest moments of fear and gratitude that really make you fall in love with her.

And if by the third act Sandra wasn't yet looked at as a force to be reckoned with in Hollywood, her final minutes in the movie mark her best acting in her early career, in which she realizes Reeves' character is going to stay on the runaway subway train with her, that he's not going to jump off and leave her by her lonesome. The relief she feels in that following moment when she discovers they're still alive feels so real and immediate that it's hard to believe that we've watched an action movie at all. It ends, after all the absurdity that's happened, as a love story!

Before *Speed* opened, Sandra was an up-and-comer, one break away from a giant movie career. After *Speed*, she finally had her pick of movie roles, starting with two lead performances she delivered with gusto in 1995. While her choice of material since making the big time has been at times questionable, *Speed* remains one of her most glorious entertainments, a movie that will continue to thrill generations of action lovers to come.

BEST SCENE
The bus jumps the fifty-foot gap!

BEST LINE
"I should probably tell you I'm taking the bus because I got my driver's license revoked." "What for?" "Speeding."

FUN FACTS

Joss Whedon did an uncredited rewrite of the script. Much of the dialogue in the finished film came from Whedon, according to screenwriter Graham Yost.

Sandra learned to drive a bus for the film, passing her test on her first attempt.

Ellen Degeneres was at one point considered for the role of Annie.

Sandra and Ian De Bont would team up three years later for the infamous *Speed 2: Cruise Control*, without Keanu Reeves at their side.

Yost and producer Mark Gordon make it clear on the *Speed* DVD audio commentary that they both had nothing to do with *Speed 2*. In fact, they weren't even invited to the sequel's premiere.

WHILE YOU WERE SLEEPING (1995)

FILM FACTS

DISTRIBUTOR: Buena Vista Pictures
PRODUCTION COMPANY: Hollywood Pictures
RELEASE DATE: April 21, 1995

DIRECTOR: Jon Turteltaub
WRITER: Daniel G. Sullivan
PRODUCERS: Roger Birnbaum, Joe Roth
ALSO STARRING: Bill Pullman, Peter Gallagher, Peter Boyle, Jack
Warden, Monica Keena, Glynis Johns

REVIEW

Once an actor hits it big, the next few choices of his or her career are extremely important. Many actors have appeared in a blockbuster, only to make five bombs thereafter, successfully ending a career before it ever really began. Sandra could have appeared in another big action movie, but she did the right thing by switching genres, and picking a project actually worthy of her talent that made us fall in love with her all over again. *While You Were Sleeping*, released in April 1995, gave Sandra her first chance to truly carry a movie, and she does so in every respect — to this day, it remains her best romantic comedy.

While it's talky, schmaltzy, and fairly predictable, *While You Were Sleeping* is one of the few comedies Sandra has made where the movie mostly exists to showcase her charm. It has a cute story, about a token booth fare collector named Lucy who saves a handsome man Peter (Peter Gallagher), whom she's fallen in love with but has never met, after he falls on the train tracks. He enters a coma, and the man's family mistakenly thinks that Lucy is his fiancée. Surprising to her more than anyone, she becomes part of the tight-knit family. To complicate things further, she starts to develop feelings for Peter's brother Jack (Bill Pullman).

While You Were Sleeping is breezy entertainment, complete with a genuinely fantastic cast. Not only is there Pullman, in his short-lived leading man phase in the mid-1990s, but there's also Peter Boyle, Micole Mercurio (Sandra's co-star in *Wrestling Ernest Hemingway*), *Mary Poppins'* Glynis Johns, and the great Jack Warden, whose scenes with Sandra are particularly warm and comforting.

While there are many positive qualities to Sandra's later romantic comedies, like *Two Weeks Notice* and *The Proposal*, nothing she's done has felt as effortless as *While You Were Sleeping*. It's not perfect by any means, and watching it today, it's easier to be more cynical about the proceedings. Most annoying of all now is that awful music score that sounds like it was bought from the upbeat cliché shop. Lucy's apartment friend Joe Jr. (Michael Rispoli) is used probably 200 percent more than he needs to be, and the amount of coincidences throughout the movie are staggering.

But if you want to turn off your brain for an hour and forty minutes, you could do a lot worse than *While You Were Sleeping*. It's probably Sandra's most likable movie, with one of her finest performances. This film marked her first Golden Globe nomination (she would go on to finally win in 2010 for her performance in *The Blind Side*), and it was also hugely popular, pulling in nearly $200 million worldwide. Julia Roberts turned the part of Lucy down, as did Demi Moore. Thank Heavens they did, because it's difficult to look at this movie thinking of anyone but Sandra in the lead role. It's her show for nearly two hours, and we wouldn't want it any other way.

1995 turned out to be nearly as good a year for Sandra as 1994, as she made not one but two blockbuster hits. By that summer, Sandra was an A-list megastar, and while *Speed* put her on the map, *While You Were Sleeping* pushed her into leading lady territory. By 1996 she was making $6 million for a supporting role in *A Time to Kill*, and in 1997, she earned a whopping $12.5 million for her Razzie-award-nominated turn in *Speed 2: Cruise Control*. But more on those movies in a bit. For now, check out *While You Were Sleeping*. It's one of the great warm-hearted entertainments of the 1990s.

BEST SCENE

Sandra reveals to the family at the wedding altar, finally, the truth.

BEST LINE

"I've had a really lousy Christmas, you've just managed to kill my New Year's, if you come back on Easter, you can burn down my apartment."

FUN FACTS

Along with her Golden Globe nomination, Sandra was also nominated for an American Comedy Award for Funniest Actress, and two MTV Movie Awards, for Best Female Performance and Most Desirable Female.

The original screenplay was about a woman in a coma and a man pretending to be her fiancé.

Nicole Kidman auditioned to play Lucy. While she didn't get the part, she did end up beating Sandra at the Golden Globes, winning Best Actress in a Comedy / Musical for Gus Van Sant's *To Die For*. Of course she would also go on to co-star with Sandra in *Practical Magic*.

THE NET
(1995)

FILM FACTS

DISTRIBUTOR: Columbia Pictures
RELEASE DATE: July 28, 1995

DIRECTOR: Irwin Winkler
WRITERS: John D. Brancato, Michael Ferris
PRODUCERS: Rob Cowan, Irwin Winkler
ALSO STARRING: Jeremy Northam, Wendy Gazelle, Dennis Miller,
Diane Baker

REVIEW

The Net might not be one of Sandra's best films, but for fans of the Oscar-winning actress, it's one of the most entertaining. While Sandra is known for her romantic comedy, action, and dramatic work, she's also made a handful of thrillers—*The Net*, *Murder by Numbers*, and *Premonition*—and *The Net* is easily the best of the lot. The movie is all Sandra all the time for its nearly two-hour running time, and it's a great joy to watch as this was really the last film she made before she launched to the A-list. Another fun element to the movie is its primitive view of the Internet, which in 1995 was only just beginning to take over everyone's lives. Sure, it's hokey and mostly predictable, but *The Net* is loads of fun, definitely one of the greatest guilty pleasures of the mid-90s.

Sandra plays Angela Bennett, a computer software analyst who works out of her home in Los Angeles, and barely sees or speaks to anybody in town, including her own neighborhood. Her only family figure nearby is her mom (Diane Baker), who (conveniently) suffers from amnesia. When she takes her first vacation in six years to Mexico, she befriends a traveling Englishman named Jack (Jeremy Northam). It turns out he's not interested in romancing her, but instead wants a computer disk that has information that could destroy his employer's company. But before he can kill her, she escapes, and wakes up a few days later, without her passport, credit cards... not even her real name. Back in the US, everyone thinks she's Ruth Marx, not Angela Bennett, and soon she starts fighting not just for her life, but also for her identity.

1995 has to be considered Sandra's best year for movies until 2000, when *28 Days* and *Miss Congeniality* both came out within a few months of each other. After the release of *Speed*, Sandra's follow-up projects needed to be films worth getting excited about. What did she give us? The charming romantic comedy *While You Were Sleeping*, followed three months later by *The Net*. Both films did better than expected at the box office and delivered on the promise of *Speed*.

The movie itself has its ups and down. Unlike her other thrillers, though, the good outweighs the bad. Take a look at 2007's *Premonition*, for example, which gives Sandra more screen-time than possibly any other movie she's made, but also gives her almost nothing to do, and no good actors to interact with. In *The Net*, which has a better, more involving story than *Premonition*, Sandra often uses her brain more than her body to solve the central mysteries of the plot, and she gets the acclaimed English actor Jeremy Northam to play off of in one riveting scene after another. The best material in *The Net* is in the first thirty minutes and the last thirty minutes, when Sandra gets to showcase how well she can captivate an audience. Very few actresses can make typing at a computer seem interesting, but Sandra somehow makes it happen. In the last two major suspense pieces of the movie, where Angela is trying to copy incriminatory files to a disk to send to the FBI, there's barely a moment to breathe for the viewer, and, even watching it from our modern world today, this sequence remains exciting stuff.

Would anyone consider *The Net* one of the better thrillers of the last twenty years? Probably not. It offers a now goofy look at the Internet circa 1995, and the plot doesn't head into any original territory—this is a basic thriller, competently shot, edited, and directed, but nothing more. It's Sandra's winning performance that saves the day, giving the movie a reason to still exist in people's minds all these years later. Sandra would go on to stumble a bit in her career in the next few years, but *The Net* marked her third major success in a row, firmly cementing her status as Hollywood's newest female superstar.

BEST SCENE
Sandra outsmarts the real Ruth Marx in her office building.

—

BEST LINE

"I don't understand… why me? Why me? I am nobody. I am nothing!"

FUN FACTS

Sandra's love interests in *Speed*, *While You Were Sleeping*, and *The Net* are all named Jack. At least they mixed it up a little in *A Time To Kill*, when the love interest was named Jake.

The game that Sandra plays at the beginning of the movie is the Apple version of *Wolfenstein 3D*.

One of the few PG-13 rated movies to use the word "fuck" in a sexual context.

The film was followed by a 1998 TV series starring Brooke Langton and a 2006 direct-to-video sequel *The Net 2.0*, starring Nikki Deloach. Neither was a success.

TWO IF BY SEA
(1996)

FILM FACTS

DISTRIBUTOR: Warner Bros.
PRODUCTION COMPANY: Morgan Creek Productions
RELEASE DATE: January 12, 1996

DIRECTOR: Bill Bennett
WRITERS: Denis Leary, Mike Armstrong
PRODUCER: James G. Robinson
ALSO STARRING: Denis Leary, Stephen Dillane, Yaphet Kotto,
Jonathan Tucker, Mike Starr

REVIEW

Sandra's first major misfire after the huge success of *Speed* was the atrocious, barely released comedy *Two if By Sea*, starring Sandra and Denis Leary as a mismatched couple being hunted by the police for stealing a painting worth millions. Dumped into theaters in early January 1996, and grossing only $10 million at the domestic box office, the movie is so awful that the studio didn't even screen it for critics. Despite decent performances from Sandra and Leary, *Two if By Sea* remains one of Sandra's weakest efforts.

It's hard to imagine that Sandra actually committed to this film after big hits like *Speed*—in every way this movie fools like something shot in the early '90s and released years later to capitalize on her success. So it's remarkable to note that she actually *pursued* the project, and was not Leary and the director's first choice. She tries her hardest in every scene to do something, anything, with this bland material, and she even sports a cute New Jersey accent, but this time, even her charm and youthful exuberance can't save a horrible screenplay. What did Sandra see in this project? She and Leary were co-stars in 1993's *Demolition Man*, so maybe they were friends at the time, and Sandra wanted to work with him again?

When asked about this film by Pete Hammond at the Santa Barbara International Film Festival in February 2010, Sandra said that part of the reason this movie failed was because of her involvement in it. Leary co-wrote the film, and he originally wrote a more offbeat, likely more interesting, script. But with Sandra in the movie, the executives at Warner Bros. wanted the film to appeal to audiences who loved her in films like *While You Were Sleeping*; thus, they watered the story down into a lame romantic comedy that has little romance or comedy.

This movie has no idea what it wants to be. The most entertaining scene is the opening, with the couple bickering back and forth in a car as a bunch of cops race toward them. If the whole movie had been like the first five minutes, a more comedic version of *Bonnie and Clyde*, with Sandra and Leary on the run from the cops, there might have been something entertaining here. And how much more fun would this movie have been if Sandra had played a more ruthless, villainous criminal on the run? A character who really went in the other direction of the innocent ones she played in her last three pictures? But instead, the two main characters settle down at a vacation home about twenty minutes in, and the movie unfolds as a dull examination of their rocky relationship.

Even diehard Sandra fans don't have much to enjoy here. There's one funny joke in the whole movie: the local police department work out of a video store. That's it. The two have little chemistry, the story goes nowhere, and the uninspired happy ending feels like another cloying moment forcibly tacked on by the studio. While the shockingly bad *All About Steve*, another comedy where Sandra rocks a weird blonde hairdo, is worse, this film is still a missed opportunity. *Two if by Sea* is something that with a different distributor and more confidence in the original script could have been something unique on Sandra's resume, but as it stands, it's her first disappointment post-*Speed*.

BEST SCENE
Sandra and Leary try to have sex in the back of their car.

BEST LINE
"Honey… SHUT UP!"

FUN FACTS

Sandra discovered she was allergic to horses while filming this movie.

Known in the UK as *Stolen Hearts*.

—

A TIME TO KILL (1996)

FILM FACTS

DISTRIBUTOR: Warner Bros.
PRODUCTION COMPANY: Regency Enterprises
RELEASE DATE: July 24, 1996

DIRECTOR: Joel Schumacher
WRITER: Akiva Goldsman (based on the novel by John Grisham)
PRODUCERS: Hunt Lowry, Arnon Milchan, Michael G. Nathanson, John Grisham
ALSO STARRING: Matthew McConaughey, Samuel L. Jackson, Kevin Spacey, Chris Cooper, Donald Sutherland

REVIEW

Sandra broke out in *Speed*, then had decent-sized hits the following year with *While You Were Sleeping* and *The Net*, but *A Time to Kill* was the first movie she made knowing she was now a major star and a known personality around the world. She's the top billed actor in a film that boasts the following powerhouse actors: Samuel L. Jackson, Matthew McConaughey, Kevin Spacey, Chris Cooper, Donald Sutherland, Brenda Fricker, Oliver Platt, M. Emmet Walsh, Kiefer Sutherland, Ashley Judd, and Charles S. Dutton. Wow! Director Joel Schmuacher was able to command a big cast of names for his movies in the mid-1990s—just look at the cast lists of *Batman Forever* and *The Client*—and *A Time to Kill* marks his best ensemble cast ever.

But Sandra, despite her being at the top of the list, isn't the lead of *A Time to Kill*—she's one of the many supporting players. Really, this is McConaughey's movie, and this marked his breakthrough role, after a series of memorable supporting turns in *Dazed and Confused* and *Lone Star*. Sandra doesn't do a whole lot in the first hour, but her character soon becomes important in the second half, serving a critical role in McConaughey's legal team. The funny thing here is that Sandra, thirty-one at the time, plays a law student, studying at Old Miss—the same school Michael Oher goes to in *The Blind Side*—but looks a good five years older than the more experienced McConaughey. This role may have suited Sandra better a few years earlier in her career, but that's a minor quibble.

The film gives Sandra opportunities to play both comedy and drama. Her begging to become a part of the defense team gives her a lot of room for cuteness, but as she becomes more involved in the case, she gets scenes of unexpected emotional power, especially in a small but memorable moment in a restaurant when she screams at McConaughey over his views on the death penalty. She unfortunately disappears for the finale, but she's featured in plenty of great scenes for a good hour and a half of the movie.

Flaws and all, *A Time to Kill* is a fine film, one of the two or three best made from John Grisham's novels. It's sprawling and messy and heartfelt, a two-and-a-half-hour courtroom thriller that works as grand entertainment. It's a shame that in all these years the film hasn't received a proper special edition home video release. A retrospective documentary, a new commentary with Joel Schmuacher, would be desirable. The DVD of *A Time to Kill* was one of the first released for the format, way back in March of 1997; the disc has to be flipped halfway through the movie just to watch the second half!

A Time to Kill would be Sandra's last blockbuster film for four years, as the rest of the '90s marked a disappointing time in her long, hit-and-miss career. It wouldn't be until Christmas of 2000, when Sandra would put on a bikini and a tiara and shimmer for an audience of hundreds in *Miss Congeniality*, that she would strike gold again. But in *A Time to Kill*, she shines, and gives one of her best performances in her early career.

BEST SCENE
Sandra lashes out at McConaughey for his position on the death penalty.

BEST LINE
"Good butt!"

FUN FACTS

Sandra was nominated for Best Female Performance at the MTV Movie Awards, and she won the Blockbuster Entertainment Award for Favorite Actress in a Suspense Film. Not quite the Academy Award yet, but it's a start.

Sandra briefly dated McConaughey, and she used him as her co-star in her directorial debut *Making Sandwiches*.

Octavia Spencer made her film debut as Sandra's nurse, and was also credited as Staff Assistant.

Kevin Costner, Alec Baldwin, and Brad Pitt were considered for the role of Jake Brigance, and Schumacher even offered his *Batman Forever* star Val Kilmer the role.

IN LOVE AND WAR
(1996)

FILM FACTS

DISTRIBUTOR: Warner Bros.
PRODUCTION COMPANY: Regency Enterprises
RELEASE DATE: December 18, 1996

DIRECTOR: Richard Attenborough
WRITERS: Allan Scott, Clancy Sigal, Anna Hamilton Phelan (based on the book *Hemingway In Love and War*, by Henry S. Villard and James Nagel)
PRODUCERS: Richard Attenborough, Dimitri Villard
ALSO STARRING: Chris O'Donnell, Margot Steinberg, Alan Bennett, Mackenzie Astin

REVIEW

Sandra has had her hits and misses throughout her career, and one of her middling misfires of the mid-90s was the earnest (no pun intended) but dull World War I drama *In Love and War*. There's a reason Sandra has never made another historical epic; she doesn't really suit the genre. She even admitted in an interview that she was in every way a chick from the '90s. (Of course, the underrated *Infamous* proved she could play historical figures. More on that film later.)

She told the Oscar-winning director Richard Attenborough before filming to make sure she didn't do any "Bullock-isms," basically saying she wanted to play the character straight and not bring any of her trademark charm and wit. Well, he listened to her, and so she gives her character almost zero personality, making for one of the least interesting characters she's played on-screen.

Chris O'Donnell plays her love interest, Ernest Hemingway, a man who spends much of the movie interested in having sex with and marrying Sandra's nurse character more than he is in working on his writing. There was a period in the mid-90s where O'Donnell appeared as the lead in a few movies (1995's *Circle of Friends* is probably the best of the bunch), and while he's OK in an ensemble, he doesn't have enough presence to carry a two-hour film. To make matters worse, he has little chemistry with Sandra.

In Love and War can be looked at as Sandra's first shot at an Academy Award (the studio gave the film a limited Oscar-qualifying run at the end of December, then released it wide a month later), but unfortunately once the reviews hit, any buzz for awards was long gone. Not that anyone can fault Sandra for taking on this project thinking some recognition could come from it; when the man who made *Gandhi* tells you he wants you to star in his next big epic, it makes sense to say yes.

The film is stilted from the start, with a brief WWI battle scene that looks like it was shot in one day on a budget half the amount needed. The next portion of the film finds Hemingway in the hospital recovering, with nurse Agnes taking care of him day and night, trying to save his leg, He starts hitting on her right away, but for the first half of the movie, she ignores him. Then, on a night when she mourns the loss of one of her patients, she finds herself drawn to him, and she (finally) kisses him. When he later comes to visit her, they have sex in an ugly brothel, of all places. Sounds like a happily ever after, right? Unfortunately, he leaves, and ultimately the two are never meant to be.

Sandra told Pete Hammond at the Santa Barbara International Film Festival that of all the films she had made, *In Love in War* was the one she wished she could go back to and do over again, knowing what she knows now. Not that anyone could blame her; most everybody in the world has forgotten about *In Love and War*. There's little drama and romance, and it has a bummer of an ending that lacks the emotional gravitas a film like this needs. After her recent successes with *The Blind Side* and *Gravity*, it seems likely she would make a better film of the same subject matter these days than the one made in the '90s—if the opportunity ever presented itself.

Ten years before the release of *In Love and War*, Sandra was getting a poisonous dart shot in her neck in her laughable film debut *Hangmen*. So by the end of 1996, one would admit she had definitely come a long way. After the huge success of that summer's *A Time to Kill*, Sandra was officially a high-profile movie star. While her career would take some bad hits over the next five years, it was safe to say that Sandra was here to stay.

BEST SCENE
Sandra slaps O'Donnell in the face.

BEST LINE
"Then close your eyes."

FUN FACTS

Sandra made *Wrestling Ernest Hemingway* three years prior. The two films are not related, although one could argue she wrestles with Ernest Hemingway in bed off-screen.

Sandra was paid $11 million for her role.

In real life, the relationship between Ernest and Agnes was never consummated, and they did not meet again after he left Italy.

Brendan Fraser tested for the role of Ernest Hemingway. He went on to play Sandra's husband in *Crash*.

SPEED 2: CRUISE CONTROL (1997)

FILM FACTS

DISTRIBUTOR: 20th Century Fox
PRODUCTION COMPANY: Blue Tulip Productions
RELEASE DATE: June 13, 1997

DIRECTOR: Jan De Bont
WRITERS: Randall McCormick, Jeff Nathanson
PRODUCERS: Jan de Bont, Steve Perry, Michael Peyser
ALSO STARRING: Jason Patric, Willem Dafoe, Joe Morton, Glenn Plummer, Colleen Camp, Tim Conway

REVIEW

Speed 2: Cruise Control is a very bad film. Certainly one of the five worst films Sandra has made in a long, mixed road of a career. Is the 1997 action flop as bad, though, as many of the blockbuster duds that have waded in and out of multiplexes all these years since? Not so much. There's a certain charm to many of those overdone summer action films of the late 1990s, a sense of fun that seems to have been erased from at least fifty percent of the summer movies we see nowadays. *Speed 2* has some of that charm at times, but it remains a major disappointment, mainly because it should have been so much better.

In the summer of 1994, the biggest surprise sensation at nationwide movie theaters was Jan de Bont's *Speed*, a rousing, kinetic action yarn that was pushed up from late August to early June to become one of the hugest hits of the year. It made a star out of Sandra, gave Keanu Reeves a jump-start to his leading man career, and allowed cinematographer-turned-director de Bont to become one of the most sought-after filmmakers of his time. The three years that followed were very kind to Sandra, with three more big hits (*While You Were Sleeping, The Net*, and *A Time to Kill*). By the time *Speed 2* was released, Sandra was a mega-star, a household name, and one of a select few Hollywood actresses who could open a movie based on her name alone.

But then everything came crashing down. If the previous winter's *In Love and War* was a disappointing misfire for Sandra, *Speed 2: Cruise Control* should go down as one of her most fatal career mistakes. While she bounced back immediately the following year with the underrated *Hope Floats*, the heavily promoted *Speed 2* became so bashed and maligned that by the end of 1997, there might have been some doubt as to whether Sandra *could* bounce back. After *A Time to Kill* opened so big, Sandra was on top of the world, and the following year should've been her time to star in a project that marked her biggest commercial success yet. Instead she gave us *Speed 2*. Without Keanu Reeves. Without a smart script. Without much... *speed*.

Sandra told Pete Hammond that she signed on for the project, traveled to the Bahamas, started shooting the movie, and kept asking the director, the producers, anyone who would listen, a pretty obvious question: "Where's a script? Can I see a script?" And apparently she never saw one, or at least, a full one. *Speed 2* does feel rushed and slapped together, like there was never much of a screenplay, but more of an outline. It's easy to imagine de Bont (who has a story credit) asking, "What if we opened on an ice cream truck chase?" Let's be honest—the opening fifteen minutes of the movie is its worst, with an action scene so awkwardly shot and constructed it feels like something from a direct-to-video movie. Worst of all, Sandra's character Annie, who never really feels like the same character from the first movie, is introduced as not just a bad driver, but literally the world's worst driver. Her cluelessness is played for laughs, but it all feels forced.

It's disheartening to think of what could have been, with a better script, with a different local, with Reeves back. It was probably impossible to make a sequel as exciting as the first film, but *Speed 2* doesn't even feel like a continuation. Sandra's Annie looks and acts different; Reeves is replaced by Jason Patric, a great actor in other productions but who is all wrong for this movie and mostly just gives blank looks throughout; the flick is PG-13, not R; and so much of the movie is goofy, versus the more serious nature of the first installment.

Another detriment is that we don't care about any of the characters on board the Seabourn Legend, while in the original *Speed* we came to know and love many of the passengers on that doomed bus. There's one action scene after another in *Speed 2*, but nothing ever gels, nothing's ever exciting. Sandra gives a rare annoying performance, Patric is a bore, Willem Dafoe does what he can with a one-dimensional villain role. Very little works.

Having said that, *Speed 2: Cruise Control* isn't a complete waste of time. While many of the action scenes ring false, the cruise ship crashing into the oceanfront town still looks awesome. While there's probably three too many dumb jokes spread throughout this sequence, it still after all these years looks extremely real. There is the occasional funny line—"What are you gonna do, Annie? Splash water on me?"—and Sandra does have some cute moments, like when she wields a giant chainsaw around, and when she has to remove a grenade from a door. Glenn Plummer returns as Tuneman from the original *Speed* for the final boat chase, this time as the owner of an expensive boat, and he gets some funny lines. Best of all, Mark Mancina's score, so memorable in the original, is given a Jamaican twist in this sequel, and despite the film's shortcomings, his score is top-notch. (The music has since been released as a Limited Edition CD that's well worth picking up.)

Speed 2 opened in June 1997 to disappointing box office and dismal reviews (although the film still ended up making nearly $150 million worldwide, and received two thumbs up from Gene Siskel and Roger Ebert). It often pops up on worst-sequels-of-all-time lists and Sandra herself has called the movie the biggest piece of crap ever made. Patric went on to have a so-so film career, and de Bont has since disappeared from moviemaking.

Sandra was the one major player to salvage her career, but no matter how many Oscars she wins, no matter how many more movies she makes, *Speed 2* will haunt her forever. As George Lopez said to Sandra at the 2010 People's Choice Awards, "You thought she couldn't top her work in *Speed 2*!" And then in February 2014, Jay Leno, in his second-to-last night hosting *The Tonight Show*, asked Sandra, "What about *Speed 2*? When you did *Speed 1*, were you automatically assigned to do the sequel?" When Sandra replied, "No," he said, "So you chose that on your own," to much audience laughter. The movie's there. She, and we, can't deny it. And while we can do our best to avoid it, it will always be there, that ugly little wart on a beautiful woman's back, a disappointing sequel to a marvelous action epic, what is universally considered Sandra's worst movie (although she made an even worse sequel eight years later with *Miss Congeniality 2: Armed and Fabulous*).

Probably the best thing that came out of *Speed 2: Cruise Control* was Sandra's desire after the fact to do better work. Despite much of the mediocrity that came out of her career over the next few years (*Forces of Nature*, *Murder By Numbers*), at least she picked smaller, more intimate projects, and would finally with *Crash* and *The Blind Side* find the kind of work she was meant to do. It may have taken another decade or so, but it would be well worth the wait.

BEST SCENE

The cruise ship crashes into the harbor.

BEST LINE

"Who's ready to par-tay on the big boat besides me?"

FUN FACTS

Sandra agreed to star in the film to get financing for *Hope Floats*.

Keanu Reeves turned down the movie to go on tour with his band Dogstar.

At the end of the movie, when the tanker truck explodes, a cow flies out with the rest of the debris, a reference to *Twister*.

Sandra's character Annie from the first film was never given a last name, but in *Speed 2*, it is revealed to be Porter.

Prior to making the film, Sandra had a fear of water.

The bus that almost hits Sandra's car in the final scene is numbered 2526. The number of the bus in *Speed* was 2525.

MAKING SANDWICHES (1998)

FILM FACTS

PRODUCTION COMPANY: Fortis Films
RELEASE DATE: 1998

DIRECTOR: Sandra Bullock
WRITER: Sandra Bullock
PRODUCERS: Sandra Bullock, Pamela Westmore
ALSO STARRING: Matthew McConaughey, Eric Roberts, Beth Grant, Octavia Spencer

REVIEW

Sandra wrote and directed a movie. Did you know that? Most people, even her super fans, probably aren't aware, because it's never been released to DVD; in fact, it's never been released on any platform. The film is *Making Sandwiches*, starring Sandra, Matthew McConaughey, and Eric Roberts, and it screened at a few festivals, like the Sundance Film Festival and the Austin Film Festival, before it quietly went away, never to be heard from again. A few people have seen it, but most of us will never get to see a frame of it: Sandra has said it was a tool for her to learn about the ins and out of filmmaking, and that it was never

—

meant to be released to the public. Not a single picture or clip has ever been released, not even on Youtube. Here's hoping it's one of those items that will show up randomly on eBay or Craigslist, but odds are Sandra herself has the only known copy in existence, and that it will never see the light of day.

The thirty-minute short, which also stars Sandra's *Speed* and *All About Steve* co-star Beth Grant, has the following tagline: "Two slices... with the world of possibility between them." Only one review has ever been posted of this film on the Internet Movie Database, which says the following: "Sandra Bullock and Matthew McConaughey make sandwiches in a small kitchen while watching television, where Eric Roberts, in drag aping his sister, reports on the weather. Short and weird." It's that word "weird" that has made this little movie a real lost treasure, especially for us Sandra fans. It's not some five-minute experimental film; it's a thirty-minute movie with two big stars, re-uniting after *A Time to Kill*. Will this movie finally re-appear one day, like Danny Boyle's *Alien Love Triangle*, which was shot in 1998 and finally released for one public screening in Wales ten years later? Anything is possible.

In an interview with Reader's Digest, Sandra said she directed the movie simply to educate herself about writing and directing a movie, and she came away from the experience deciding that she didn't have the talent to succeed in either of these disciplines. While Sandra has produced multiple movies over the years, she has never since written or directed any films, and it's unlikely she ever will. Sandra has been notably her best when she's hired as the actress, and only the actress. Take 2009 for example. She only acted in *The Blind Side*, the film that was her biggest critical and financial success up to that time and netted her the Academy Award for Best Actress. What's the film she produced in 2009? *All About Steve*, the movie that netted her the Razzie for Worst Actress.

But still, despite her proclamation to never write and direct a film again, this short oddity *Making Sandwiches* languishes out there in the universe like an undiscovered love letter from youth. After the screening at the Austin Film Festival, it hadn't been seen or heard about since, until an August 2011 interview with *The Help* star Octavia Spencer brought up the short film and Sandra for being the triggers that jump-started her career. Spencer appeared in *A Time to Kill* as Sandra's nurse, and then Sandra hired her for a small part in *Making Sandwiches*. Spencer had apparently agreed to help only in the casting of the short film, but soon found herself sharing scenes with Sandra and McConaughey. Sandra also brought up Spencer and the short film when she accepted her Hollywood Film Award in 2013 for *Gravity*: "Only in Hollywood can a PA become an actor in fifteen minutes, and then go on to win an Academy Award, like she did." Spencer said her work in *Making Sandwiches* ultimately launched her career, because the tape got her an agent.

Wait. So there *is* a tape of *Making Sandwiches* somewhere out there, possibly collecting dust at the bottom of a talent agent's bottom drawer somewhere? For those of us Sandra fans, *Making Sandwiches* remains the "lost" movie, the one least likely to ever surface for our viewing pleasure, and to

—

give us opportunities to find a **Best Scene** and a **Best Line**. But if it ever does get a release, officially or unofficially, it will be an event almost as exciting as the latest Sandra feature. So come on people, start checking your drawers, cabinets, and local garage sales, and let's find this movie. It has to be out there somewhere… right?

FUN FACTS

The only film Sandra wrote and directed.

The only project Sandra has been affiliated with that has never been released to the public.

The only time Sandra and McConaughey have worked together since *A Time to Kill*.

HOPE FLOATS
(1998)

FILM FACTS

DISTRIBUTOR: 20th Century Fox
PRODUCTION COMPANY: Fortis Films
RELEASE DATE: May 29. 1998

DIRECTOR: Forest Whitaker
WRITER: Steven Rogers
PRODUCERS: Lynda Obst; Sandra Bullock (executive producer)
ALSO STARRING: Gena Rowlands, Harry Connick Jr., Mae
Whitman, Cameron Finley

REVIEW

After the critical and financial failures of *In Love and
War* and *Speed 2: Cruise Control*, it was time for a career
make-over for Sandra, or, at the very least, a better received
film. Sandra didn't follow up those two movies with
another big action movie or end-of-the-year awards-bait
production; instead, she made the surprise 1998 hit *Hope
Floats*. And while it's not a great film, it offered Sandra her
first meaty dramatic role.

Coming on board as executive producer for the first
time in her long career, Sandra learned the ropes of film
producing by working with Lynda Obst (*One Fine Day*,

Interstellar). After the disaster that was *Speed 2*, Sandra wanted more control over her projects. In an interview on the set of *Hope Floats* in 1997, Sandra stated that she was saying "yes" to too many projects she didn't believe in, and that she would now be making one movie a year, maybe. (Of course that wasn't the case; she would make six films over the next three years.) *Hope Floats* was a project she obviously believed in, because she signed on to *Speed 2* partly to ensure that 20th Century Fox would allow her to make the intimate drama. Probably the most surprising statistic is that *Speed 2* earned $48.6 million nationwide, while *Hope Floats* made $60 million; nobody in 1997 would have predicted that!

Hope Floats is a frustrating movie because there are occasional scenes of emotional truth, but they are surrounded by such a low-key, predictable story that it's hard at times to care about the outcome. The title itself is lame, and a lot of the film, directed by the better-actor-than-director Forrest Whitaker, is way too schmaltzy for its own good. The most maudlin moments occur when Whitaker slow-mos certain shots so that we as an audience will take note that what's happening on screen is *very dramatic*. The second-to-last scene, involving Sandra discovering a picture of Harry Connick Jr. and walking up to him on the street outside, is particularly hokey.

The most interesting aspect to *Hope Floats* is its opening few minutes, which is tonally different than the rest of the film. We're introduced to Sandra's Birdee character at an appropriately cheesy Jerry Springer-like talk show hosted by the where-the-hell-did-she-go Kathy Najimy. Birdee learns on the show that her high school sweetheart husband Bill (Michael Pare) has been cheating on her for over a year with her best friend (a well cast Rosanna Arquette) and that he doesn't love her anymore. This wild opening makes the movie feel like it's going to be a comedy in the vein of *Miss Congeniality* or *The Proposal;* instead, the rest of the film finds Birdee trying to rediscover herself and make a new life for her and her daughter (Mae Whitman, by far the film's MVP), with little in the way of high-stakes comedy. It's unusual to say the least; it's like if *While You Were Sleeping* opened with a scene of Lucy not being chosen on *The Dating Game*, or if *Crash* opened with Jean screaming at a bunch of black guys on an episode of *Maury*. The purpose of the opening scene is to reveal to Birdee that her husband is an adulterer. There were fifty other ways to get that idea across, and it seems odd that the screenwriter went with this one.

The rest of the movie has its flaws, but it also has effective moments. Sandra is surrounded by a terrific supporting cast, including Gena Rowlands and Whitman, as well as a who's-who of character actors (Connie Ray, who starred alongside Sandra in *Speed 2*, is a stand-out). The storylines involving Birdee's relationship with her mother and with her daughter are authentic and involving, mostly due to the fine performances. The scene where Birdee lashes out at her daughter on the staircase comes to mind, as does the scene in the bathroom, where she drunkenly cowers over a toilet and cries to her mom about how much she misses her husband and how lost she is without him.

Hope Floats hasn't gained much of a following in the years since it's been released; Sandra's fans would probably still pick *Speed*, *While You Were Sleeping*, and *Miss Congeniality* as her best films made in 2000 or prior. And, shockingly, there are probably more fans of the overrated *Practical Magic*, made the same year. But while it's an imperfect, sometimes overly sentimental film, *Hope Floats* was an important stepping stone in Sandra's career, not just as an actress, but as a producer as well.

BEST SCENE
Sandra cries drunkenly to Rowlands about her husband.

BEST LINE
"Childhood is what you spend the rest of your life trying to overcome."

FUN FACTS

The first major motion picture made under Sandra's production company, Fortis Films.

Rowlands and Sandra both graduated from the same high school, Rowlands in 1947, Sandra in 1982.

Rosanna Arquette's role as Birdee's friend Connie went uncredited.

The film's dance sequences were choreographed by Patsy Swayze, mother of Patrick Swayze.

—

Sandra won Best Actress at the 1999 Lone Star Film & Television Awards, and Mae Whitman won Best Performance in a Feature Film at the 1999 Young Artist Awards.

PRACTICAL MAGIC (1998)

FILM FACTS

DISTRIBUTOR: Warner Bros.
PRODUCTION COMPANY: DiNovi Pictures, Fortis Films
RELEASE DATE: October 16, 1998

DIRECTOR: Griffin Dunne
WRITERS: Robin Swicord, Akiva Goldsman, Adam Brooks
PRODUCER: Denise Di Novi
ALSO STARRING: Nicole Kidman, Aidan Quinn, Stockard Channing,
Dianne Wiest

REVIEW

Practical Magic is a film that has two tremendous qualities—Sandra and Nicole Kidman, as sisters. When this project was first announced in 1997, it sounded like a sure thing. How in the world could anyone screw up a movie with these two dynamic actresses playing witches? Well, you have Akiva Goldsman (*Batman & Robin*) co-write the script, and you give Griffin Dunne, a better actor than filmmaker, the directing reigns. While the film has its fans, *Practical Magic* is mostly a waste of concept and talent. It's not a terrible movie, not near Sandra's worst, but the consistent mediocrity is what makes the film so frustrating.

On the DVD audio commentary, the producer and director both say that their favorite scene is the "Midnight Margarita" scene that takes place halfway through the film, but this scene highlights everything that is wrong with *Practical Magic*: nobody knows what it's supposed to be. It starts whimsical, with a delightful prologue, leading to some cheesy but fine scenes in the first fifteen minutes. But then the movie takes an abrupt turn when Sally (Sandra) goes to save her sister Gillian (Kidman) from her sordid lifestyle and accidentally kills one of her lovers. This event sets off the silly conflict of the rest of the movie, but it's ultimately treated as a device to bring Sally closer together with a private investigator (Aidan Quinn).

There were so many places to take this movie. Imagine what a director like Guillermo Del Toro would have done with these actors and this material. The story that the producer and director apparently wanted to tell was a murder mystery, mixed in with a hokey love story that never takes off because Sandra and Quinn have little chemistry. Worst of all? There's not much magic in *Practical Magic*! It's alluded to a lot, and there are a few scenes where the two sisters, and sometimes their aunts (Stockard Channing and Dianne Wiest), perform a spell or two. But not until the very end do we get any real magic, and it's only used to eradicate an evil spirit out of Gillian. *Hocus Pocus* this movie shouldn't have necessarily been, with Sandra and Kidman hamming it up for ninety minutes, dancing and singing and riding on broomsticks. But a more specific vision, a creative point of view, could have turned this from a lackluster disappointment to a memorable late '90s guilty pleasure.

Sandra said in a press junket for *Practical Magic* that one of the greatest things to happen to her in her career was the failure of *Speed 2*, because it meant that she could finally pursue smaller projects that she was more interested in rather than big action blockbusters. Unfortunately, in this case, a smaller project doesn't always mean better. One of the few joys of *Practical Magic* is that it's Sandra's movie, more than it is Kidman's, and she has the occasional funny moment. But the film just never comes to life. *Practical Magic* began Sandra's mediocre period, with movies like *Forces of Nature* and *Murder by Numbers* not doing her career any favors. We certainly are still a long way from *Gravity*.

BEST SCENE
The final scene, when the family in witch hats jump off the roof of their house.

BEST LINE
"It was the curse, wasn't it! He died because I loved him so much!"

FUN FACTS

After bad test screening reactions, composer Michael Nyman's score was rejected for sounding too European. It was replaced with a score by Alan Silvestri. The change was made so late that the first batch of soundtrack CDs had Nyman's score on it.

According to Sandra in the DVD commentary, in the margarita scene, she and Kidman actually did get drunk.

For the final scene, the entire population of the real town was invited to show up in costume and appear as townsfolk.

In 2010, Warner Bros. and ABC Family attempted to develop a television series based on this film. To date, it hasn't been produced.

THE PRINCE OF EGYPT (1998)

FILM FACTS

DISTRIBUTOR: Dreamworks SKG
PRODUCTION COMPANY: Dreamworks Animation
RELEASE DATE: December 18, 1998

DIRECTORS: Brenda Chapman, Steve Hickner, Simon Wells
WRITERS: Philip LaZebnik, Nicholas Meyer
PRODUCERS: Penney Finkelman, Sandra Rabins
ALSO STARRING: Val Kilmer, Ralph Fiennes, Steve Martin, Martin Short, Michelle Pfeiffer

REVIEW

Big A-list casts for animated movies is the norm now, but in the early 1990s and earlier, such was not the case. Take one of the greatest animated films of all time, *Beauty and the Beast*. The most famous person in that voice cast is still probably Angela Lansbury. *Aladdin* has Robin Williams but no other major stars. Even *The Lion King* is packed more with characters actors than A-listers.

The Prince of Egypt, the first animated feature from Dreamworks, was designed to be a big, blockbuster awards contender at the end of 1998, and Jeffrey Katzenberg, who had been trying to get the movie made when he was working at Disney, certainly pulled out all the stops when it came to the voice cast. Look at this list of actors—Val Kilmer, Ralph Fiennes, Steve Martin, Martin Short, Helen Mirren, Jeff Goldblum, Michelle Pfeiffer, Danny Glover, and Mel Brooks. If those actors weren't enough, Dreamworks threw in one more big star for one of the voice roles—Sandra.

Steven Spielberg, David Geffen, and the aforementioned Katzenberg founded Dreamworks in 1994, and one of the ambitions of the studio was to create the kind of animated features that could stand proudly alongside and even outdo the ones coming out of Disney. While Disney had another golden age of animation from 1989 to 1994, starting with *The Little Mermaid* and ending with *The Lion King*, the studio by the end of the decade was churning out more forgettable fare, like *Hercules* and *Mulan*. *The Prince of Egypt* couldn't have arrived at a more proper time. Dreamworks was betting a lot on the movie's success, releasing it just a week before Christmas.

But did it live up to the enormously high standards? Definitely not. With a production budget of $70 million (before marketing and advertising costs), the movie made about $100 million in the United States, and received only two Academy Award nominations, for Score and Song. The reviews were mixed, and the audience reaction, tepid. It's clear in looking at the film again after all these years that the filmmakers' ambitions could only take them so far. The movie has a well-constructed opening sequence and a fabulous closing one, with two memorable songs interspersed throughout; however, the majority of the movie is a ferocious bore.

Sandra shows up about thirty minutes into the movie. She plays Moses's sister Miriam, who bumps into her brother and tries to convince him he is not a born Prince of Egypt but just another common man. She's not in the film much—she has one other extended scene toward the end the movie—but it's a treat to hear her voice in animated form. To date Sandra has not appeared in any other animated film, so why did she commit to *The Prince of Egypt* in the first place? Two words: Steven Spielberg. He called her back in 1994 and asked her if she would play Miriam. I imagine she didn't have to think too hard before she gave him her answer.

BEST SCENE
The parting of the red seas.

BEST LINE
"I know to whom I speak, Aaron! I know who you are. And you are not a prince of Egypt!"

FUN FACTS

The Prince of Egypt remains the only voice work Sandra has done for a major motion picture, but she will finally return to the animated world in 2015, when she offers her voice to *The Minions*, a *Despicable Me* sequel, playing the film's villain, Scarlett Overkill.

Katzenberg constantly pitched the idea of *The Prince of Egypt* to the Walt Disney Company while he was there, but Michael Eisner didn't like the idea.

The film was followed by a direct-to-video prequel, *Joseph: King of Dreams*, in 2000.

Only five actors did both the singing and speaking parts of their characters: Ralph Fiennes, Michelle Pfeiffer, Martin Short, Steve Martin, and Ofra Haza. Sandra's singing voice was provided by Sally Dworsky, as well as briefly by the film's director, Brenda Chapman.

Until 2001, *The Prince of Egypt* was the most expensive animated feature ever.

FORCES OF NATURE (1999)

FILM FACTS

DISTRIBUTOR: Dreamworks SKG
PRODUCTION COMPANY: Roth-Arnold Productions
RELEASE DATE: March 19, 1999

DIRECTOR: Bronwen Hughes
WRITER: Marc Lawrence
PRODUCERS: Susan Arnold, Ian Bryce, Donna Roth
ALSO STARRING: Ben Affleck, Maura Tierney, Steve Zahn, Blythe Danner, David Strickland

REVIEW

The mediocre train of Sandra's career continues. Starting with 1996's underwhelming *In Love and War*, Sandra had a string of movies for the next few years that were underwhelming at best and abysmal at worst. Most will probably remember *Speed 2*, but few will remember the contrived road trip romantic comedy *Forces of Nature*. Released in March 1999, the movie hasn't exactly aged well. And while it's not a complete mess—Sandra actually has a unique character to play here, unlike her flavorless role in *Practical Magic*—the movie suffers from a stupid story, poor casting, unfunny jokes, too many coincidences, and a lack of chemistry between the leads.

It's easy to see what attracted Sandra to this character—it's unlike any she had played before. Sarah Lewis is an erratic free spirit who dresses wildly and speaks anything and everything that's on her mind. When we first see her, she's making out with a total sleazebag who looks like he's been dealing dope since the age of three. Her hair has purple steaks, her clothing is black and tight, and she has enough eye shadow to cover her entire face. After playing less flawed characters, ones who are always likable and firmly planted on the ground, Sandra, if nothing else, got the opportunity here to play someone different.

The plot of *Forces of Nature* surely had to be inspired partly by John Hughes' 1987 comedy gem *Planes, Trains, and Automobiles*, as both films are about a man trying desperately to get home for an important occasion, while an eccentric fellow traveler keeps causing him trouble and prevents him from reaching his destination in a timely fashion. In the case of *Forces of Nature*, a conservative goodie-good Ben Holmes (Ben Affleck) is trying to get from New York to Savannah for his wedding to a faithful, beautiful woman (Maura Tierney), but his plane crashes, he finds other means of transporation, and the unstable Sarah becomes his unwanted travel mate. Will he make it to his wedding? Will he even want to, with Sarah now in his life? And do we care?

The quality of this movie can be summed up by a Matt Damon quote in Kevin Smith's *Jay and Silent Bob Strike Back*. Playing themselves, Affleck makes fun of all the "girly" roles Damon took in 1999 and 2000 (like *All the Pretty Horses* and *The Legend of Bagger Vance*), but then Damon strikes back with, "I take it you haven't seen *Forces of Nature*." While the director of *Forces of Nature*, Bronwen Hughes, who later transitioned to television work, definitely tries to give the movie a distinct and sometimes effective visual style to separate it from other romantic comedies of the time, the movie suffers from more simple matters. Sandra is fine in the movie, but she seems about ten years too old for her role, and she has zero chemistry with Affleck, who basically has a blank stare throughout the movie. Even worse, he plays such a bland dweeb of a character that we as viewers lose interest in him pretty fast. If the film had been all about Sandra's character, and her quest to reunite with her son, there might have been something here.

In a 2010 interview with Charlie Rose, Sandra said that she quit film acting in 2002 for two and a half years because she wasn't happy with her work. While Sandra has never discussed *Forces of Nature* in any major interviews since the film's release, it's appropriate to assume this movie is one she would consider among the work she's not proud of. During the film we discover that Sarah hasn't seen her son in ten years, and at the end their reunion has the potential to be a rare honest moment. Unfortunately, it's handled so saccharine—the boy immediately warms up to her as if she's been coming over every weekend—that the Sarah story's conclusion doesn't offer effective closure.

Forces of Nature isn't Sandra's worst film, but it's certainly one of her most forgettable. Sandra gives the wild role her all, but unfortunately she's paired with a leading man who looks like he'd rather be anywhere else, as well as an absurd plot that may be the most contrived in her entire filmography. Thankfully the road of her career would take a positive turn in the year 2000, but at the end of 1999, Sandra was at a crossroads.

BEST SCENE
Sandra and Affleck officially meet on the airplane before it crashes.

BEST LINE
"Why didn't I think of that when I was unconscious and bleeding from the head?"

FUN FACTS

Screenwriter Marc Lawrence went on to write *Miss Congeniality 1* & *2* for Sandra, as well as *Two Weeks Notice*, his directorial debut.

The producers had been looking for a Sandra Bullock "type" for the role of Sarah. Finally, they ended up just asking Sandra herself!

Matthew McConaughey presented Sandra with her Teen Choice Award for Choice Hissy Fit. She was also nominated for Favorite Actress – Comedy/Romance at the Blockbuster Entertainment Awards, but lost to Drew Barrymore for *Never Been Kissed*.

GUN SHY
(2000)

FILM FACTS

DISTRIBUTOR: Hollywood Pictures
PRODUCTION COMPANY: Fortis Films
RELEASE DATE: February 4, 2000

DIRECTOR: Eric Blakeney
WRITER: Eric Blakeney
PRODUCER: Sandra Bullock
ALSO STARRING: Liam Neeson, Oliver Platt, Mitch Pileggi, Mary
McCormack, Frank Vincent

REVIEW

It started with *Hope Floats*. Sandra had been interested in producing from an early point in her career, but not until she learned from Lynda Obst on 1998's *Hope Floats* did she start making a claim to her new role in the industry. Even her biggest fans would admit that Sandra's film work in the late '90s is not some of her best, and she knew that if she produced more of her own films, she could have more control over her work. After producing her short film *Making Sandwiches* and executive producing *Hope Floats*, she finally took on her first project as sole producer—the mob comedy, *Gun Shy*.

Quietly released in limited release in February 2000, *Gun Shy* is one of the lesser known Sandra films. While it stars Liam Neeson, Oliver Platt, and Sandra, in a small role, the movie is rather bland and unremarkable. It also hasn't aged well, feeling like it was shot in the early '90s. The writer/director Eric Blakeney has gone on to write and direct... nothing, and Neeson practically sleepwalks through his part. There are some mildly funny moments, and the quirky story has promise, but the film never takes off.

Neeson plays an undercover DEA agent who is trying to take down a Columbian cartel and a New York mob family. He seems confident on the outside but inside he's suffering from gastrointestinal problems, a character quality that doesn't exactly make for exciting viewing (unless you like watching an attractive actor like Neeson poop every few minutes). This condition leads him to visiting the beautiful "enema Queen" played by Sandra. This is probably the only movie made in which the boy and girl have a Meet Cute through colonic irrigation, so *Gun Shy* at least has that going for it. Platt also has fun with a cheesy mob boss role, and gives the proceedings a much-needed jolt of energy.

The main problem with the movie is that it tries to do too much. It tries to be a mob flick, a romantic comedy, an action film, a psychological study. Unlike other films that successfully combine genres, *Gun Shy* never knows which way to go, which makes for a frustrating viewing experience. And unfortunately for Sandra fans, her part in the movie is limited and rather unnecessary; the romantic subplot feels tacked on and thrown in simply to get her in the movie.

While it must be commended that Sandra was able to get her first feature film project as sole producer off the ground, *Gun Shy* is not her best work. Sandra would go on to produce the much better *Miss Congeniality* later the same year, but the majority of her success in the following decade would be her dramatic acting in films like *Crash*, *Infamous*, and *The Blind Side*, and not her producing projects.

It must be said, however, that even though *Gun Shy* isn't top rate, the soundtrack, which Sandra also produced, is fantastic. It features music by James Brown, Los Lobos, Push Stars, and Bob Schneider, whose music video "Round & Round" featured Sandra in a cameo. Also, Sandra's own mother Helga Bullock, who passed away a few weeks after *Gun Shy* was released, has a haunting track on the CD titled "Caro Mio Ben."

BEST SCENE
Sandra gives Neeson an enema.

BEST LINE
"Lucky Charms, magically delicious!"

FUN FACTS

With a budget of $10 million, *Gun Shy* ended its box office run with only $1.6 million.

At one point in the film, Sandra boards a bus numbered 2525, a clever reference to *Speed*.

Richard Schiff, who appeared in a small part in *Speed*, plays Elliot in this film. He was also in *Forces of Nature*.

28 DAYS
(2000)

FILM FACTS

DISTRIBUTOR: Columbia Pictures
PRODUCTION COMPANY: Tall Trees Productions
RELEASE DATE: April 14, 2000

DIRECTOR: Betty Thomas
WRITER: Suzannah Grant
PRODUCER: Jenno Topping
ALSO STARRING: Viggo Mortensen, Dominic West, Elizabeth
Perkins, Margo Martindale

REVIEW

2000 was a solid year for Sandra, one of the best in her career yet. She made three decent to great films in 2000, producing her first feature with *Gun Shy*, delivering her best dramatic performance to date in *28 Days*, and producing and starring in the blockbuster hit *Miss Congeniality*, which has since become one of the definitive goofy comedies of the early 2000s. She would star in three more films again in 2002, to middling success; in 2009, she also had three films released, but despite starring in two of her biggest hits, she still had to account for the disastrous *All About Steve*. No, 2000 was a great year for Sandra, and while *28 Days* is in no way a masterpiece, it's a solid film that gave Sandra her most complex role to date.

The best material in *28 Days* is its opening twenty minutes, when Sandra, playing an alcoholic thirty-something named Gwen, races to her older sister's wedding, accidentally destroys the wedding cake, then drives a limo straight into a house. We immediately transition to a significant time later, when she arrives at a rehab clinic. She's cranky and bitter and hates to be there, but when she faces potential jail time, knowing that both her physical and mental health are deteriorating, she finally starts to change into the person she was always meant to be—a smart, sober person with the capability of leading a happier life.

These early moments—of Gwen drinking and going wild, and of dealing with the early aftermath of her painful detoxing—allow the actress to stretch her acting muscles more than she ever had up until that point. *In Love and War* was Sandra's first starring role in a drama, but the film didn't allow her to create an interesting character, while *Hope Floats* was the first drama she made that allowed her to showcase highs and lows of emotions on screen. But *28 Days* is arguably the first film Sandra made that showed us what she would be capable of down the road in films like *Infamous*, *The Blind Side*, and *Gravity*.

One of her best scenes in *28 Days* takes place in front of her counselor's office. Director Betty Thomas allows the action to play out mostly in one long take, as Gwen shakes and begs the man (a low-key Steve Buscemi) to let her stay at the clinic and not be transferred to the local prison. It's a heartbreaking scene that rings true. She's also fantastic in a brief, well-constructed scene that finally brings her and her older sister (Elizabeth Perkins) together, with her trying not to cry until she can't hold the tears in anymore.

The movie as a whole, however, never fully comes together, and too much of the later half falls flat. The movie is chockfull of great actors, especially, as her eccentric British boyfriend, Dominic West—with whom Sandra has terrific chemistry. Unfortunately, when the film enters its second hour, there's too much going on, with Gwen flirting with bad boy Eddie (Viggo Mortensen), a long-ish subplot that goes nowhere, and Gwen trying to enrich the pained life of her soap-opera-obsessed roommate (Azura Skye), a subplot that ends in tragedy but then is never referenced again. While the opening scenes are fresh and funny, so much of the later part of the film gets bogged down in too many storylines and characters and revelations, and after awhile it all starts to look and feel like a TV movie, especially with the corny happy ending involving Gwen raising a horse's hoof.

28 Days has its flaws, and, like *Gun Shy*, the movie hasn't aged very well. But it's entertaining enough, especially the first half. If you can survive the never-ending Mortensen subplot and the longwinded and lame soap opera spoof, you'll enjoy one of Sandra's more effective dramatic performances. The material could have been stronger—a surprise given that Susannah Grant, who wrote the fantastic *Erin Brockovich*, penned the script—but *28 Days* is still worth a second look for Sandra fans.

BEST SCENE

Sandra crashes a limousine into a house.

BEST LINE

"I'm having the worst damn day of my whole damn life! So
if it isn't too much to ask of you people, will you back the
fuck off!"

FUN FACTS

Sandra won the 2000 Bambi Award for Best Film –
International.

Sandra spent time in a rehab clinic to prepare for this role.

Sandra drank a triple espresso before any scene that
required her character to have uncontrollable shakes.

MISS CONGENIALITY (2000)

FILM FACTS

DISTRIBUTOR: Warner Bros.
PRODUCTION COMPANY: Fortis Films
RELEASE DATE: December 22, 2000

DIRECTOR: Donald Petrie
WRITERS: Marc Lawrence, Katie Ford, Caryn Lucas
PRODUCER: Sandra Bullock
ALSO STARRING: Michael Caine, Benjamin Bratt, Candice Bergen,
William Shatner

REVIEW

Sandra began the year 2000 by producing her very first movie—*Gun Shy*—and ended the year by acting in her still most successful film to date that she also produced—*Miss Congeniality*. In a constantly surprising career that has included action, comedy, mystery, and romance, Sandra has truly done it all, but most of her fans would probably single out *Miss Congeniality* as one of her best movies, not just because of how fun of it is, but also because it's one of her rare films that fully showcases her comedic talent.

With a lackluster cast, the movie could have been a terrible direct-to-video trifle, but with Sandra playing FBI

Agent Gracie Hart, and with a surprisingly strong roster of supporting players, *Miss Congeniality* is often very funny, and it still holds up well. While the 2005 sequel remains one of her worst movies, the original is an entertaining laugh riot that is easily one of Sandra's best comedies.

While *Miss Congeniality* is a tad long at nearly two hours—and could have been even longer, with director Donald Petrie revealing in his commentary track that subplots involving Gracie Hart's mom and dad were both axed in the cutting room—it is never dull, and even its lengthy finale at the Miss United States Pageant is filled with another action and surprises to keep things moving swiftly.

Sandra was nominated for a second Golden Globe nomination for *Miss Congeniality* (losing to Renee Zellweger for *Nurse Betty*), and it's easy to see why: she gets to play an unattractive, sloppy FBI agent in the film's first reel, and the moments before the ugly duckling is transformed make for Sandra's funniest moments, with her gifts for comedy put fully on display. Just the way she eats her ice cream at the bar, snorting and slurping to great effect, makes for plenty of laughs, and her first scene with Caine not only sets up plenty of punch-lines for later but also makes for great comedic chemistry. Sandra is always at her best when she's paired with on-screen talent who can match her, and Sandra got one of her best gifts with Caine in this movie—their relationship gives the comedy an unexpected heartbeat.

Miss Congeniality has become one of those staples on Sunday afternoon TBS and TNT marathons, the kind of movie you turn on halfway through and end up watching all the way until the end. It's no masterpiece of comedy, but it's frothy and fun, and gives Sandra one of her most memorable comedic roles. After starring in and producing this film, she worked again with the writer Marc Lawrence on his 2002 directorial debut *Two Weeks Notice*, but *Miss Congeniality* remains the movie that best represented the duo's audience-friendly comedic sensibilities.

BEST SCENE

Having-a-bad-hair-decade Sandra meets the gay, super classy Caine at a posh New York restaurant.

BEST LINE

"I am in a dress, I have gel in my hair, I haven't slept all night, I'm starved, and I'm armed! Don't mess with me!"
falls

FUN FACTS

The boxing scene in Gracie's home was completely ad-libbed by Sandra.

Sandra and Bratt did all their own fighting.

"I'm gliding here!" is a parody of the famous line, "I'm walking here!" from *Midnight Cowboy*.

Miss Congeniality grossed $212 million worldwide, making for one of Sandra's biggest hits up to that time.

For this film, Sandra won the American Comedy Award for Funniest Actress in a Motion Picture, the Blockbuster Entertainment Award for Favorite Actress – Comedy, and the Teen Choice Award for Film – Choice Wipeout.

GEORGE LOPEZ
(2002-2007)

TV SHOW FACTS

DISTRIBUTOR: ABC
PRODUCTION COMPANY: Fortis Productions
PREMIERE DATE: March 27, 2002

DIRECTOR: Joe Regalbuto (38 episodes)
WRITERS: Robert Borden, George Lopez, Bruce Helford (creators)
PRODUCERS: Sandra Bullock, Frank Pace, George Lopez, Jim Hope
ALSO STARRING: George Lopez, Constance Marie, Valente
Rodriguez, Belita Moreno

REVIEW

Before we examine the rest of Sandra's film work, let's
take one last look at her television career post-*Speed*. Prior
to her fame, she didn't shy away from TV work. She
appeared in the *Lucky Chances* mini-series in the early '90s,
and even headlined her own show, a thirteen-episode
reworking of the Oscar-winning 1988 film *Working Girl*.
Once she hit the big time with *Speed* and *While You Were
Sleeping*, she stayed focused on film work, but from 1994 to
2002 she came back to television here and there, with a few
funny cameo appearances. Ultimately, though, Sandra's real
stamp on TV came not as an actress, but as a producer, for

the very successful *George Lopez*, which lasted six seasons and 120 episodes on ABC.

Sandra received her first executive producer credit on *Hope Floats*, and she solely produced her first two features in 2000, with the underperforming *Gun Shy* and the huge box office hit *Miss Congeniality*. Around this time that Sandra was finding her producing groove, she approached a little-known Hispanic comedian named George Lopez after seeing one of his stand-up comedy routines and asked him if he would be interested in headlining a comedy show. Sandra was concerned with the lack of Hispanic-oriented shows on American television and wanted to get a sitcom on the air that starred this minority without being exclusively about the Hispanic American community. Picked up in 2002, the show was a big hit for ABC, and it went on to garner a lucrative syndication deal, making Sandra a cool $10 million.

When Sandra was asked what she did when she didn't work for that two and a half year hiatus between *Two Weeks Notice* and *Miss Congeniality 2*, she often said she was busy producing *George Lopez*. And busy she was! Not only was she working behind the scenes, but she often appeared on the show as well, as the slapstick character Accident Amy, a stumbling, disheveled, wackier version of Gracie Hart. It's pretty juvenile comedy, but if you like watching Sandra bumping her head a lot, it's good, clean fun. She appeared in three episodes—"Happy Birthdays" and "No Free Launch" in 2002, and "Bachelor Party" in 2004.

In addition to *George Lopez*, Sandra also appeared as herself on two memorable occasions. Her episode on the short-lived ABC show *Muppets Tonight*, in which she spoofs the plot of *Speed* and goes nuts as various characters, is a true hidden gem for Sandra fans. She has still never hosted an episode of *Saturday Night Live*, and her turn on *Muppets Tonight* is the closest she has come to hosting a variety show. Not every sketch works, but her performance as an eccentric therapist singing with Kermit the Frog is delightfully zany and well worth checking out.

Another brief spot of hers worth searching for is her cameo on the short-lived Fox show *Action*, which starred Jay Mohr and Buddy Hackett. In the episode titled "Blowhard," she played a subversive version of herself. She shows up at the film executive Peter's door, a wee bit upset that he has been circulating around town a VHS tape, called *While You Were Sleeping… On My Face*, that features him and Sandra having sex. It's a fun few minutes of Sandra ridiculing her girl-next-door public image, and kicking some serious ass.

BEST SCENE
Sandra sets her arm on fire.

BEST LINE
"My leg broke my fall."

FUN FACTS

The character George Lopez was ranked #18 in TV Guide's 2004 list of 50 Greatest TV Dads.

The show won one Emmy Award in its entire run, for Outstanding Art Direction.

Muppets Tonights aired on ABC, and lasted two seasons and twenty-two episodes. Other hosts included Michelle Pfeiffer, Billy Crystal, Tony Bennett, Martin Short, Pierce Brosnan, and Paula Abdul.

Sandra's episode of *Muppets Tonight* was scheduled to air on April 19, 1996, but producers realized it was the one-year anniversary of the Oklahoma City bombing, and felt an episode with a bombing plot (a parody of *Speed*) was inappropriate. The episode aired two months later.

Action aired on Fox, and lasted one season and thirteen episodes. Other notable cameos included Sandra's *Speed* co-star Keanu Reeves, as well as Salma Hayek, David Hasselhoff, and Tony Hawk.

MURDER BY NUMBERS (2002)

FILM FACTS

DISTRIBUTOR: Warner Bros.
PRODUCTION COMPANY: Shroeder Hoffman Productions
RELEASE DATE: April 19, 2002

DIRECTOR: Barbet Schroeder
WRITER: Tony Gayton
PRODUCERS: Richard Crystal, Susan Hoffman, Barbet Schroeder;
Sandra Bullock (executive producer)
ALSO STARRING: Ryan Gosling, Michael Pitt, Ben Chaplin, Agnes
Bruckner, Chris Penn

REVIEW

Before she won an Academy Award for *The Blind Side*, Sandra rarely won or was nominated for any significant awards, and few critics ever gave her kudos for her dramatic range. But one thing that's rarely written about her is the chances she takes on new genres. In 1996 she followed a legal thriller with an historical drama. In 1998 she followed a tearjerker drama with a fantasy comedy. In 2000 she followed a rehab drama with a slapstick comedy, and if *Miss Congeniality* taught us anything, it's that we love Sandra when she's silly and fun.

So naturally it would have made sense for Sandra to follow up *Miss Congeniality* with another no-brainer comedy, right? No, that would have been too easy. Sandra had three films released in 2002, all fairly mediocre in their own specific ways, but all completely different in tone and genre, and, if nothing else, at least that element should be recognized for her versatility. *George Lopez,* which Sandra produced, was also launched that year, so 2002 has to be considered one of Sandra's busiest years in the industry, so much so that after she wrapped *Two Weeks Notice,* she took a two-and-a-half year break from acting.

Murder by Numbers, which was screened out of competition at the Cannes Film Festival, was her first film released in 2002, and it's noteworthy for a few reasons. One, she plays a character named Cassie with a profession similar to Gracie's in *Miss Congeniality,* except this time she plays the role totally straight. Second, while in the majority of her movies Sandra is the star, in this she is one of three—Michael Pitt and Ryan Gosling take over half the story, as two high school students committing grisly murders, seducing girls, and manipulating Cassie for their own personal pleasure. And third, and most noteworthy of all, the scenes in *Murder By Numbers* that truly sparkle with energy and vitality are the ones *not* with Sandra's character, but with Pitt and Gosling.

Cassie is fairly basic and, can it be said, by the numbers? Her backstory and development feel very TV-movie-of-the-week, in that her arc is fairly obvious from the start. Pitt and Gosling on the other hand are magnetic in their quiet, eerie scenes, showcasing the kind of talent we'd be exposed

---

to in the exciting years to come. Pitt would go on to deliver impressive performances in *The Dreamers*, *Funny Games*, and *Boardwalk Empire*, while Gosling would earn an Oscar nomination for *Half Nelson*, and excel in films like *Drive*, *Blue Valentine*, and *The Place Beyond the Pines*. If there's anything memorable about *Murder by Numbers*, it's the performances by Pitt and Gosling. Kudos have to be given to Sandra for taking on a movie that doesn't entirely focus on her, and instead gives two up-and-coming actors a shot.

BEST SCENE

The erotically charged encounter between Sandra and Gosling in front of her car.

BEST LINE

"The profile doesn't fit the profile!"

FUN FACTS

The moment near the end of the movie, where Gosling licks Sandra's face, was not scripted. After a few takes, Gosling asked Sandra if it would be okay if he added it in to prove his character's sick nature.

The title refers to the song, "Murder by Numbers," written by Sting and performed by The Police.

Todd Field, Oscar-nominated actor and director, played a murder suspect, but his scenes were deleted.

DIVINE SECRETS OF THE YA-YA SISTERHOOD (2002)

FILM FACTS

DISTRIBUTOR: Warner Bros.
PRODUCTION COMPANY: Gaylord Films
RELEASE DATE: June 7, 2002

DIRECTOR: Callie Khouri
WRITERS: Callie Khouri (based on the novel by Rebecca Wells);
adaptation by Mark Andrus
PRODUCERS: Bonnie Bruckheimer, Hunt Lowry
ALSO STARRING: Ellen Burstyn, Ashley Judd, Maggie Smith, James
Garner, Cherry Jones, Angus Macfadyen

REVIEW

Just six weeks after the release of *Murder by Numbers*,
Divine Secrets of the Ya-Ya Sisterhood opened in theaters to
modest acclaim and better-than-expected box office. As
much as high-powered male executives are wary of making
movies for a female audience, these kinds of films always

tend to do well, even when they're on the mediocre side, like this film.

Divine Secrets of the Ya-Ya Sisterhood is ambitious, blending flashbacks with the present and presenting themes of parental neglect, abuse, racism, and alcoholism. The movie tries to be both a family drama and a broad comedy, and it doesn't fully succeed at either. On the plus side, first time director Callie Khouri (who won an Academy Award for her *Thelma & Louise* screenplay) assembled a tremendous cast, which includes Ellen Burstyn (who was hot off her Oscar nomination for *Requiem for a Dream*), Ashley Judd, Maggie Smith, and, of course, Sandra. If nothing else, it's fun to spend two hours watching these gals play around and try to elevate fairly routine material.

Sandra originally didn't want to play the role of Siddalee Walker, a playwright who accidentally reveals in a printed interview all the secrets of her eccentric mother Vivi (played in the present by Burstyn, and in flashbacks by Judd). In the audio commentary, Khouri reveals that Sandra was tired after shooting *28 Days*, *Miss Congeniality*, and *Murder by Numbers* nearly back to back, and wanted to take a break. But Khouri begged and pleaded, and finally Sandra reconsidered. What's interesting is that Sandra would go on a few months later to shoot *Two Weeks Notice*, and then she finally *did* take her vacation, a two-and-a-half year vacation. When asked about her long break years later, Sandra said she looked at the work she'd been doing and wasn't too happy with it. Odds are *Divine Secrets* was included in that list, not because it's a bad movie, but because it's such a forgettable one.

The best material in the film isn't the Siddalee section at all, but the flashbacks to Vivi as a young woman. These scenes aren't anything spectacular, but at least they have the occasional instances of raw emotion. In the present day scenes, a lot of the comedy is too over-the-top to work well, and the only laugh-out-loud moments come from Smith, who gets the best one-liners ("It took me twenty-five years to find out my husband was gay"). Sandra does the best she can with what she's given to do. The early scene of her talking to her mother on the phone is memorable, but once she gets stuck in a cabin for the middle chunk of the movie, she just basically lays around in her PJs and reminisces about the old days. Not exactly exciting.

So much of *Divine Secrets of the Ya-Ya Sisterhood* reminds the viewer of 1996's *A Time to Kill*. Why? *Divine Secrets* was based on a bestselling novel, as was *A Time to Kill*. One of the subjects it deals with is racism, like *A Time to Kill*. Most of the film is set in the south, like *A Time to Kill*. *Divine Secrets* reteamed Sandra and Judd, who co-starred in *A Time to Kill*, and in both films, they never act in one scene together! And lastly, almost eerily, the same tune is featured prominently in important scenes: "Take My Hand, Precious Lord."

Overall, while 2002 was a year filled with a lot of Sandra, only her third film of the year—*Two Weeks Notice*, with Hugh Grant—could be described as actually *good*. *Divine Secrets of the Ya-Ya Sisterhood* is a more interesting film than the lackluster thriller *Murder by Numbers*, and unfortunately, like that film, the best material in *Divine*

Secrets is without Sandra. We Sandra fans are always happy just to see her on the screen, even if it is in a dreadful mess like *Premonition* and *All About Steve* (more on those later), but whenever possible, we prefer her in good movies. We know when Sandra is presented with a solid script and a good director that she can be great, but, like in the case of *Divine Secrets of the Ya-Ya Sisterhood*, she doesn't always have the best material to work with.

BEST SCENE
Sandra receives a phone call from her disgraced momma.

BEST LINE
"I don't want to get all scrappy!"

FUN FACTS

Bette Midler was one of the executive producers.

Sandra was nominated for a Teen Choice Award for Choice Actress, Drama/Action Adventure.

The film was based on the Rebecca Wells novel, as well as its prequel collection of short stories, *Little Altars Everywhere*.

TWO WEEKS NOTICE (2002)

FILM FACTS

DISTRIBUTOR: Warner Bros.
PRODUCTION COMPANY: Fortis Films
RELEASE DATE: December 20, 2002

DIRECTOR: Marc Lawrence
WRITER: Marc Lawrence
PRODUCER: Sandra Bullock
ALSO STARRING: Hugh Grant, Alicia Witt, Dana Ivey, Robert Klein

REVIEW

It was supposed to be Sandra's ultimate romantic comedy. First, there was *While You Were Sleeping*, still to date Sandra's best rom-com. She went on to make other films that weren't full on romantic comedy but had strong elements of them—*Two if by Sea*, *Forces of Nature*, and *Gun Shy*. After the release of *Two Weeks Notice*, Sandra said she was done with the genre (even though she would go on to make another one in 2009, with *The Proposal*). She had worked with the best in Hugh Grant, after all, and had allowed her frequent writing collaborator Marc Lawrence to direct her for his first time. In looking at *Two Weeks Notice* all these years later, how has the movie held up?

It's fine. It was fine in 2002 and it's fine today, with a handful of scenes that put a smile on your face, and decent chemistry between the two. At the time, the film was noted as the first to shoot in New York City after the 9/11 terrorist attacks, and the location serves the movie well. What doesn't serve the movie as well is its obvious plot, which we know from the first "meet-cute" between Sandra and Grant what exactly is going to happen. She's an activist named Lucy who works hard to save legendary buildings from destruction. He's a rich playboy named George who doesn't care about these buildings and will gladly knock another one down to make a quick buck. She starts working for him, and she realizes over the course of many months that he's never going to change. Will he change, though? And will he decide at the late hour that he's in love with her? Gee, let me guess.

There was potential for something greater here, but unfortunately it was written and directed by Marc Lawrence, who hasn't exactly had the best track record. His first collaboration with Sandra was on *Forces of Nature*—not the best sign—and the only movie they worked on that turned out better than expected was *Miss Congeniality*. But Lawrence is also responsible for the insipid sequel *Miss Congeniality 2: Armed and Fabulous*, as well as the later lackluster Hugh Grant efforts *Music and Lyrics* and *Did You Hear About the Morgans?* His resume reads like a late night spent in movie hell. In this regard, *Two Weeks Notice* works as well as it does due to the charm of the two stars. Put

Sandra and Grant in humorous situations, and you're bound to get some entertainment value out of it. They work well together, so much so that it would be interesting to see the two work together again under the hands of a more assured director, and with a more imaginative screenplay.

As the movie stands, it's an occasionally amusing trifle, and not much more. The most memorable scene takes place when Lucy has to desperately use the bathroom, in a freeway packed with parked cars no less, and ultimately does her business in the back of a dirty RV. It's something we rarely see a big star like Sandra do on screen, and, unfortunately, it's a moment some of us can relate to. The finale is predictable and not as romantic as it could have been, but the very last scene, which takes place in Lucy's apartment, is terrific, the kind of spontaneous moment that the movie should have had more of throughout its 100-minute running time.

So is *Two Weeks Notice* Sandra's ultimate romantic comedy? It's the kind of mediocre entertainment that would be fine to watch late at night on TBS if nothing else is on, but it's not half of the movie the funnier *The Proposal* is, and it has nowhere near the charm and pleasure and romance of *While You Were Sleeping*. *Two Weeks Notice* isn't bad, but it could have been better.

BEST SCENE

Sandra eats one too many chili dogs and finds the urge to go to the bathroom while stuck in a massive traffic jam.

BEST LINE

"No, actually, this is for two."

FUN FACTS

Two Weeks Notice was Sandra's third solo outing as a producer, following *Gun Shy* and *Miss Congeniality*. This was another hit for Sandra, grossing about $200 million worldwide.

Sandra's name is Lucy in both *While You Were Sleeping* and *Two Weeks Notice*. She also orders Chinese food in both from Mr. Wong.

Donald Trump and Norah Jones appear as themselves.

Sandra's *Miss Congeniality* co-star Heather Burns returned here, playing her close friend Meryl.

MISS CONGENIALITY 2: ARMED & FABULOUS (2005)

FILM FACTS

DISTRIBUTOR: Warner Bros.
PRODUCTION COMPANY: Fortis Films
RELEASE DATE: March 24, 2005

DIRECTOR: John Pasquin
WRITER: Marc Lawrence
PRODUCERS: Sandra Bullock, Marc Lawrence
ALSO STARRING: Regina King, Ernie Hudson, Eileen Brennan, William Shatner

REVIEW

Sandra is not known for always making the best movies in the world. For the longest time, every good movie she made seemed to be followed by a bad one. For every *The Proposal*, there's an *All About Steve*, which earned Sandra the Razzie for Worst Actress. For every *The Net*, there's *Premonition*, her ridiculous 2007 thriller that is definitely one of her all-time lows. And for every *Speed*, there's, of course, *Speed 2: Cruise Control*. But *Speed 2* isn't Sandra's worst sequel. The worst sequel she ever made is the one where she's sporting a Vegas drag costume and impersonating incontinent old ladies. Yes, I'm talking about 2005's disaster, *Miss Congeniality 2: Armed and Fabulous.*

To make matters worse, this embarrassing movie came out after a two-and-a-half year absence from the screen for Sandra, when we fans were clamoring for something, anything, from her. After making 2002's *Two Weeks Notice*, she took a sabbatical from filmmaking, one that was supposed to be six months but ending up being more than two years. (She spent time producing *George Lopez,* and remodeling old buildings in Austin, Texas.) So what was her big come-back movie after this longer-than-desired break? The unquestioningly bad *Miss Congeniality 2*. Did Sandra learn her lesson with *Speed 2*? Even Sandra herself has gone on talk shows and talked about how awful the action sequel was. She's never, however, been very outspoken about her other sequel, which is in much more need of a few heartfelt apologies.

The film begins decently; in fact, the very first scene is the best. Sandra returns as Gracie Hart, who's prettier and better dressed, but still the same old Gracie. Trouble ensues while she's trying to stop a bank robbery, when her cover is blown by a fan who wants her autograph. She can't just stay back in the shadows any longer; her mission at the Miss United States pageant has captured the nation's imagination. Therefore, her boss (Ernie Hudson) suggests that instead of having her continue to work in the field that she become the face, celebrity, and cheerleader of the FBI. Soon Gracie's signing copies of her new book and chatting with Regis Philbin on his talk show. She becomes a shallow version of her former self, just at the moment that last year's Miss USA winner Cheryl (Heather Burns), along with Stan Fields (William Shatner) get kidnapped. Oh, and then there's Regina King as Gracie's sassy sidekick.

Miss Congeniality 2: Armed and Fabulous isn't just awful because of its tired plot, or because it has one unfunny scene after another, or because it includes Sandra's most unpleasant character in a film ever (Gracie is really self-centered in this sequel); this one's particularly bad because of its obvious laziness. The 2000 original isn't anything remarkable, but it's funny and breezy, and it ranks as one of Sandra's best comedies. (It also has Michael Caine, who's sorely lacking this time around.) This sequel just has nothing going for it. Not only is the main character shallow for a good eighty percent of the running time; there's not a story here worth telling, not a relationship worth exploring. The whole endeavor is just a big, dumb commercial, a tasteless McDonalds product if you will, hoping to steal hard-earned dollars from the movie-going public. Sandra is better than this.

Thankfully the ensemble drama *Crash* opened just six weeks after *Miss Congeniality 2: Armed and Fabulous*, and managed to wash away a lot of the bad aftertaste of one of her worst movies ever. For even the most die-hard Sandra fans, *Miss Congeniality 2* was not a good time at the movies, but thankfully *Crash* would show us all a hint of the greatness that was to come.

BEST SCENE
Benjamin Bratt (off-screen and unheard) breaks up with Sandra over the telephone.

BEST LINE
"Is it the snorting? Cuz I don't have to snort."

FUN FACTS

To date, Sandra's final collaboration with Marc Lawrence.

Sandra won Choice Movie Actress: Comedy at the Teen Choice Awards.

The film grossed $101 million worldwide, less than half of what the first film made.

In *Miss Congeniality*, there was supposed to be a storyline where Gracie's mother was killed in the line of duty. The storyline was included in the sequel.

A "Miss Congeniality" poster can be seen in the background at the Las Vegas airport during the scene where Gracie is supposed to be flying back to New York.

To date, Sandra's second and last sequel.

CRASH
(2005)

FILM FACTS

DISTRIBUTOR: Lions Gate Films
PRODUCTION COMPANY: Bob Yari Productions
RELEASE DATE: May 6, 2005

DIRECTOR: Paul Haggis
WRITERS: Paul Haggis, Robert Moresco
PRODUCERS: Don Cheadle, Paul Haggis, Mark R. Harris, Cathy Schulman, Bob Yari
ALSO STARRING: Don Cheadle, Matt Dillon, Thandie Newton, Terrence Howard, Brendan Fraser

REVIEW

Sandra needed *Crash*.

Over the years, even Sandra's biggest fans had to admit that she wasn't picking the finest scripts or choosing the most talented directors or working in the kinds of genres that fully showcased what she had to offer. Since her breakout in *Speed*, Sandra had appeared in a handful of Oscar friendly movies, like *A Time to Kill* and *In Love and War*, but nothing she made from 1994 to 2004 necessarily set awards season on fire. She made some fun comedies and decent dramas, but where was the breakthrough we fans were hoping for? Who would give Sandra a chance to shine not just as a deft comedienne, but as a fine dramatic actress? The answer to that question was writer/director Paul Haggis.

It was exciting to hear the news in late 2003 that Sandra had joined an ensemble drama, even though there were no expectations for the kind of movie *Crash* would become. Would it be a masterpiece a la *Magnolia*, or a forgettable film like *Crossing Over*? For nearly a year, news on the production was minimal. Between *Two Weeks Notice* and *Miss Congeniality 2*, she worked on *Crash* for four days in Los Angeles, flying herself out to the set and shooting inside director Haggis's own home. She would spend months filming other movies, and less than a week on this one. Could *Crash* really be the breakthrough she needed? In every sense, yes!

Sandra is not in very much of the film. Featured in five scenes, one of which lasts barely thirty seconds, she's in it less than most of the other major actors. Matt Dillon and Thandie Newton received the most acclaim, and Sandra wasn't nominated for any major acting awards, only sharing in the Screen Actors Guild ensemble win that pushed the movie forward toward its controversial Best Picture win over *Brokeback Mountain* at the Academy Awards. This was the first time, however, that directors of a higher caliber finally witnessed what Sandra was capable of, especially with a strong script and a chance at doing something different.

When does Sandra play unlikable? Not often. When had she ever played a demonizing racist who spews nothing but vulgarities out of her mouth? Her first scene in the film is routine, but her second is revolutionary, the kind of sixty seconds of screen-time that literally revamps an entire career. Her scene in the hallway at her home, when her character Jean demands that her husband (Brendan Fraser) change the locks again in the morning because she's scared the Hispanic locksmith will go out and sell the keys to his friends, is electric acting against type. You see the pain in her eyes, you know that she's been molded into this person throughout many years of increasing solitude, but it's still shocking. Sandra is a big star and might not have wanted to be seen in this kind of dismal light. But she commits one hundred percent to this character and this scene, and shows us for the first time the kind of dramatic power she's capable of.

Her other great scene in *Crash* takes place in one long tracking shot, when she talks to a "friend" on the phone as she tries to reason why she wakes up every morning angry and bitter. The scene starts casually, but then slowly transforms into one of intense sadness. We all have felt her kind of rage from time to time, and Sandra shows how this negative energy can weigh down a person's spirit day after day.

Crash premiered at the Toronto Film Festival in 2004 to minimal press, then got what appeared to be a quiet release, in the first week of May 2005. The film received decent to good reviews and quickly disappeared, only to resurface at the end of the year as screeners from Lions Gate started making the rounds. Awards didn't look to be in the cards for *Crash*—it barely registered with nominations at the

Golden Globe awards. But after it won Best Ensemble in a Motion Picture at the Screen Actors Guild Awards, it earned multiple Academy Award nominations, including Best Picture, Director, Screenplay, and Best Supporting Actor for Dillon. It wasn't the prestige factor that won *Crash* all its awards—nobody making the low-budget film at the time probably thought any significant acclaim was in store two years later—but the tone, the feeling, the overwhelming emotion of the movie ultimately registered with voters, and audiences, around the world. Is *Crash* deserving of a Best Picture Oscar? No. It's not half the film *Magnolia* is, P.T. Anderson's ensemble film from 1999 that wasn't even nominated for Best Picture, and it hasn't lasted the way *Brokeback Mountain* has. But it's a solid film, one that benefited many of the actors, like Terrence Howard and Dillon, and certainly Sandra.

Sandra has still made some bad movies since *Crash*, but the quality certainly saw a noticeable uptick. Without her acclaimed performance in *Crash*, would we have had her overlooked turn in *Infamous*? Would John Lee Hancock have pursued her so hard for *The Blind Side*? Would she have appeared in a Stephen Daldry film, or starred in a space epic directed by Alfonso Cuaron? It's all possible, but those few minutes of dramatic intensity she delivered in *Crash* finally, thankfully, catapulted her to another level.

BEST SCENE

Sandra lashes out at Fraser about wanting the locks changed.

"This time it'd be really fucking great if you acted like you actually gave a shit!"

FUN FACTS

Sandra has less than six minutes of screen-time in the entire film.

Sandra was so committed to appearing in the film that she bought her own plane ticket to fly to the set.

Crash holds the distinction for being the last Best Picture Oscar winner to be released on VHS in the United States, and the first to be released on Blu-ray.

John Cusack was the original choice for the role of District Attorney Rick Cabot, which eventually went to Brendan Fraser.

The film was followed by a 2008 TV series with the same title. Lasting thirteen episodes, the series starred Dennis Hopper, Sandra's *Speed* co-star.

LOVERBOY
(2006)

FILM FACTS

DISTRIBUTOR: Think Film
PRODUCTION COMPANY: Bigel / Mailer Films
RELEASE DATE: June 16, 2006

DIRECTOR: Kevin Bacon
WRITER: Hannah Shakespeare (based on the novel by Victoria Redel)
PRODUCERS: Kevin Bacon, Daniel Bigel, Michael Mailer, Kyra Sedgwick
ALSO STARRING: Kyra Sedgwick, Kevin Bacon, Matt Dillon, Marisa Tomei, Dominic Scott Kay

REVIEW

Easily the most obscure film Sandra has made since *Speed* is the 2006 drama *Loverboy*, starring Kyra Sedgwick, Matt Dillon, Oliver Platt, and Marisa Tomei, and directed by Kevin Bacon. The film received an extremely limited release in theaters before it quietly disappeared into the bottom of DVD dollar bins. Telling the story of a neglected daughter named Emily, who years later becomes a possessive mother, *Loverboy* is a moderately entertaining but mostly unremarkable film. So why is it even being discussed in this book? Sandra has a small but pivotal role as Mrs. Harker, a neighbor of young Emily (Sosie Bacon).

She is featured in two flashbacks. In the first, she rubs a bruise on Emily's leg and walks her to the school bus. Wearing a morning bathrobe and sporting a big and wild hairdo, she acts in her first minutes of screen-time the kind of sexily confident character she rarely plays in the movies. In the second scene, she chats with Emily on her lawn and plants on her a big wet kiss. Lit like the early morning sun is beaming down on them, and with a yellow filter applied to the scene, Sandra has rarely looked so luminous. Her screen-time amounts to barely three minutes in the entire film, but her quiet, tender performance is effective nonetheless.

Loverboy premiered at the Sundance Film Festival in January 2005, then had a limited run in Los Angeles and New York in June 2006. During this latter time, I attended a screening at the Arclight Hollywood, where the director Bacon was in attendance for a Q&A following the film. It was a packed house of moviegoers who were probably more interested in seeing Bacon in person than seeing the movie itself, and the Q&A did not disappoint, going for at least thirty minutes. He answered questions about the look of the film, the origins of the film, but all I cared to ask was the obvious: how and why did he get Sandra for this super brief role? "I was really impressed with Sandra Bullock's performance," I said to Bacon, who sat quietly up on the stage. "I was just curious how she came to be in the movie." Bacon answered that he was friends with Sandra, and that he called her out of the blue and asked her if she would come out to New Jersey and play a part in his theatrical directorial debut. He said that she only worked two days on the movie and that he too enjoyed her performance and what she brought to the role.

What is most notable about Sandra's participation in *Loverboy*, as well as in *Crash*, is that she is not afraid to take a small part in a film if she believes in it. This was the stage in Sandra's career when she was passing on romantic comedies and mediocre scripts in order to revamp her career, and while *Loverboy* didn't make much of an impression at the time, for Sandra die-hards it offers a compelling character, Mrs. Harker, who is unique enough to warrant a longer subplot, or maybe even her own movie.

BEST SCENE
Sandra sits on her front lawn with her wheelchair-bound son.

BEST LINE
"Don't let any boys give you trouble, okay? All you have to remember is that deep down inside, they're all afraid of girls."

FUN FACTS

Loverboy opened in limited release on June 16, 2006, the same day that *The Lake House* opened nationwide.

The film grossed only $30,000 at the box office.

Actors in the film include Bacon's wife Kyra, his daughter Sosie, his son Travis, and his brother-in-law Robert. Also, Bacon's brother Michael provided the music score.

Sandra's name or likeness was not featured in any of the movie's advertising, including the theatrical trailer.

THE LAKE HOUSE (2006)

FILM FACTS

DISTRIBUTOR: Warner Bros.
PRODUCTION COMPANY: Village Roadshow Pictures
RELEASE DATE: June 16, 2006

DIRECTOR: Alejandro Agresti
WRITER: David Auburn (based on the motion picture *Il Mare* aka
Siworae, written by Eun-Jeong Kim and Ji-na Yeo)
PRODUCERS: Doug Davison, Roy Lee
ALSO STARRING: Keanu Reeves, Christopher Plummer, Dylan
Walsh, Shoreh Aghdashloo

REVIEW

For fans of the original *Speed*, the announcement of a romantic drama called *Il Mare* was one eleven years in the making. I remember that morning well. It was in early 2005, and I was in my sophomore year dorm room at Loyola Marymount University. I clicked over to comingsoon.net, probably my favorite of all the movie news sites, and saw this headline at the top of the news stories: "Sandra Bullock and Keanu Reeves Re-Team for *Il Mare*." I clicked on the article, read through it at least twice, and danced around my dorm room to Kool and the Gang's "Celebration."

Over the years, Sandra has had solid chemistry with some of her leading men—Bill Pullman in *While You Were Sleeping*, for example—but the best chemistry she ever had with one of co-stars was Keanu Reeves in *Speed*. Jason Patric? Chris O'Donnell? Harry Connick Jr.? No, thanks. If she were to ever re-team with one of her co-stars, I hoped it would be Reeves. Of course I wanted them to reunite for *Speed 2*, but Reeves passed, and opted to perform with his band instead. Most people applauded him for avoiding the critically dissed sequel, but everyone would likely agree that the sequel would've been far better if he had returned. Chemistry is something unexplainable, something that can't be planned. Sandra and Reeves have it. And I hoped for years that they'd find another project to do together. In 2006, that project was *Il Mare*, later retitled *The Lake House*.

For fans of Sandra, and especially those who enjoy seeing Sandra and Reeves together, there's a lot to admire and cherish in *The Lake House*. Unfortunately, in the years since its release, it's difficult to categorize this film as anything but disappointing. Of course the main disappointment is obvious—they only spend a few minutes actually together on-screen. Why hype their return to a film if they spend the whole thing apart? But this core letdown wouldn't matter if the film itself was a great one, and while it's not a bad movie, *The Lake House* is often too slow, and too precious, when it could be soaring. Watching it again after all these years, I was reminded just how dull the middle hour of the movie gets, and how when the movie focuses on anything but getting the two main characters together, the narrative drags.

First, let's get the bad out of the way, so we can focus on the good, because while *The Lake House* is not the film it could have been, there are some interesting elements to be found here. Some may call the worst part of *The Lake House* the whole time travel element, which, yes, is a bit silly. But time travel in a film's narrative is a device you either go with or laugh at, and often I just go with it. It's not the time travel that doesn't work so well in *The Lake House*; it's in the deadly serious nature the movie deals with it. Alex (Reeves) and Kate (Sandra) come to learn that their mailbox has the ability to transport letters, as well as anything else that can fit, back and forth in time, two years apart—and yet they treat this miracle as if the mailbox was recently painted with pretty colors. There's literally no excitement or enthusiasm given toward this incredible happening! This is an element of the story that I didn't really think about when I saw it the first time in 2006, but it was at the forefront of my mind upon this later viewing. The subplots in the movie don't really add much either, like Alex's relationship with his dying father (Christopher Plummer), who isn't developed enough to gain much interest in. Kate's on-and-off boyfriend (Dylan Walsh) and Alex's sort-of-girlfriend (Lynn Collins) are total blanks, and only a couple notches above cardboard cutouts.

And then there's the central, glaring paradox of the movie, which if actually analyzed makes no sense. Alex is killed in 2006 while walking across the street to get to Kate, and then on that same day two years later Kate learns that the man who died that day was Alex. Therefore, she goes back to the lake house and writes him a letter, telling him to stay away from her for two years, to wait for her, and to come find her that very day. Magically, he does show up just a few seconds later, not dead, and very much alive. Sandra and Reeves' final kiss is so passionate and wonderful you can almost forgive the lame-brained logic. But when you think about it, the ending doesn't work, because of this paradox: If Kate literally watched Alex die two years ago, how could he still be alive two years later?

Aside from these problems, however, there is a lot to enjoy in this film. The production design and cinematography are top-notch, with that striking house on the lake specifically built for the film, and with gorgeous photography of Chicago in both the summer and winter. There is a beautiful sequence where Alex and Kate go on a walk together, two years apart, in the windy city. Just the way the director Alejandro Agresti shoots the film is really striking in its sometimes dream-like quality. The performances by Sandra and Reeves, aside from the previously mentioned quibble about their apathy toward the plot's time travel element, are great, and this film, after *Crash*, continued Sandra's trajectory toward finding better material.

That last scene, when they finally find each other and he plants on her one of the greatest, wettest kisses in film history, *is* a great one (again, beautifully shot), but the best scene in *The Lake House* takes place about halfway through, when Alex meets Kate for the first time in his timeline, in 2004. She doesn't know who he is yet, of course, but he's been writing to her for months. She says a quick hello to him at her surprise birthday party, then gets to talking to him on her front porch. The director Agresti does something extraordinary here, especially for a mainstream wide-release movie: he allows Sandra and Reeves to just sit together and talk, in one take, for three whole minutes. For someone who had waited twelve years to see these two together again on-screen, I found this one simple take to be like magic. And the ensuing scene where they dance to Paul McCartney's "This Never Happened Before" is just as hypnotic. While the film has problems as a whole, this segment works wonders.

Finally, did anyone notice the various nods to *Speed*? The first is that Reeves' name in the film is Alex, which was the name of Annie's boyfriend in *Speed 2*, played by Jason Patric. The second is that the dog that at one point belongs to both Alex and Kate is named Jack, which was Reeves' name in the original *Speed* (Sandra did indeed call the dog this to reference the 1994 action movie). And the whole movie revolves around an accident in which Reeves' character is hit by—what else—a *bus*! The film tonally couldn't be any different from *Speed*, but the nods are definitely there.

Will Sandra and Reeves ever make another movie together? On the interview circuit for *The Lake House*, they both said they would love to do a third film, if the right script ever landed in their laps. It's been almost a decade since *The Lake House*, and they're not getting any younger. Here's hoping for one more film starring Sandra and Reeves, one that's hopefully not *The Lake House 2*, or—yikes—*Speed 3*. *The Lake House* is decent entertainment, but these two deserve something extraordinary.

BEST SCENE

Sandra and Reeves chat on the front porch, then dance on the grass.

BEST LINE

"It's kind of a long distance relationship."

FUN FACTS

Sandra revealed that the title house had running water but no toilets.

The Lake House was the first movie to be released simultaneously on DVD, HD DVD, and Blu-ray.

Sandra and Reeves won Choice Liplock at the 2006 Teen Choice Awards.

The name of the exclusive restaurant in the film is Il Mare. This is the name of the International title of the Korean film *The Lake House* was based on.

John Cusack was the first choice for the role of Alex, but he declined. He turned down Brendan Fraser's role in *Crash* as well. Does the man not want to work with Sandra?

INFAMOUS
(2006)

FILM FACTS

DISTRIBUTOR: Warner Independent Pictures
PRODUCTION COMPANY: Killer Films
RELEASE DATE: October 13, 2006

DIRECTOR: Douglas McGrath
WRITER: Douglas McGrath (based on the book, *Truman Capote: In Which Various Friends, Enemies, Acquaintances, and Detractors Recall His Turbulent Career*, by George Plimpton)
PRODUCERS: Jocelyn Hayes, Christine Vachon, Anne Walker-McBay
ALSO STARRING: Toby Jones, Sigourney Weaver, Jeff Daniels, Daniel Craig, Gwyneth Paltrow

REVIEW

When Sandra walked onstage at the 85th Annual Academy Awards in 2013, stunning in a black Elie Saab cap-sleeve gown, she was introduced, as, how else, "Oscar winner Sandra Bullock." For too many years Sandra kept picking the wrong projects, kept working with the wrong directors, and we fans hoped an opportunity would come along that would finally showcase her true talent. She had her moments in *Hope Floats* and *28 Days*, but the first dramatic film that really opened up directors' eyes to what she could do dramatically was *Crash*, which went on to win the Oscar for Best Picture. In 2010, just four years after *Crash*'s big win, she finally received her first Oscar nomination and award, for *The Blind Side*. But is *The Blind Side* Sandra's golden achievement? Is *Crash*? No.

Until *Gravity*, Sandra's best dramatic performance on film was in the little-seen and mostly ignored 2006 film *Infamous*, in which she stars as the famed Pulitzer Prize-winning author Harper Lee. Why was this film ignored to the extent it was? It had nothing to do with the quality of this film; it is truly an outstanding, expertly crafted picture about Truman Capote's writing of his most famous book, *In Cold Blood*. No—*Infamous* was ignored because the film *Capote*, about the exact same subject matter, was released a year before to great critical acclaim, multiple Oscar nominations, and an Oscar win for the late Philip Seymour Hoffman.

When *Infamous* opened just six months after that year's Oscar telecast (the same one in which *Crash* had its big victory), nobody cared. While people saw both *Deep Impact* and *Armageddon*, and both *Antz* and *A Bug's Life*, they embraced *Capote*, yet pretended like *Infamous* didn't exist. It's a shame because while *Infamous* treads on the same territory, it approaches the subject matter with a different angle, bringing in more of Truman's life in New York and allowing room for humor. It boasts a tremendous cast that includes Gwyneth Paltrow, Sigourney Weaver, Jeff Daniels, and Daniel Craig, pre-James Bond. Most of all, Toby Jones' performance as Truman Capote is astounding, just as good as Philip Seymour Hoffman's and possibly even better, since he closer resembles the real Capote in his physicality. If *Infamous* had been released a year before *Capote*, Jones would have been guaranteed an Oscar nomination, no doubt, and even Sandra herself might have been up for her first nomination as well. She's that good in this film.

Catherine Keener was nominated for an Academy Award for playing Harper Lee in *Capote*, but does anyone remember that performance? Sandra makes a much more memorable impression in *Infamous*, with her subtle, natural turn as the famed literary giant—she also, if you check out old photos of the *To Kill a Mockingbird* author, looks almost exactly like her. Truman Capote surrounded himself with New York's richest socialites, but he also remained close with one childhood friend—Ms. Lee. In the film Truman is so intrigued by the story of a deadly shooting in middle-of-nowhere Holcomb, Kansas, that he enlists his friend Harper to accompany him to the town to investigate the story for a potential long-form article, which of course became the acclaimed book, *In Cold Blood*. It is this riveting section of the movie that Sandra has the most screen time.

Jones and Sandra don't make for an on-screen duo that would necessarily scream great chemistry, but they are terrific together, radiating a warm, natural friendship that really does feel like it goes back decades. There is an interesting dynamic between the two, Sandra with her mousy hair and lack of make-up and reserved behavior, and Jones with his spot-on voice and crazy outfits and showy demeanor. There are plenty of scenes of Sandra in the first third of the film where she doesn't say a word but simply listens, to Jones, to stories, to the characters she meets in the small town. It's a fascinating change of pace for an actress who normally is the center focus of the narrative.

Does she have a big "Oscar" scene in the movie? The film integrates interviews with its characters throughout, and Sandra gets not one but two great moments to tell stories about Truman. But it's one of her final scenes in Kansas, when she confronts Truman for using his ways of fiction to tell the dark true story of the brutal murders, that gives her the best chance to shine. With her perfected Alabama accent, a cigarette between her fingers, and obvious disdain for what Truman is trying to accomplish, she nails this hard-to-watch argument between two old friends, with both sides offering views that make sense. It's a scene like this one that Sandra shows just the kind of actress she can be, when she's met with the right script, director, and character.

For Sandra fans, *Infamous* is one of those movies of hers that might have fallen through the cracks. She's not the lead, it's not a comedy, it didn't receive any acclaim or awards consideration. But all these years later, not having the former 2005 film *Capote* to consider, it's much easier to admire *Infamous* for the magnificent film that it is. Writer/director Douglas McGrath, whose previous credits include *Emma* and co-writing the script to Woody Allen's *Bullets Over Broadway*, made wise choices with his ensemble cast, but especially with Sandra, who rarely plays a role this tender, this observant. As her career finally started taking a sharp turn for the better, with meatier roles and more complex dramatic fare, this film provided Sandra her most interesting role on screen to date. She may have won the

Academy Award for *The Blind Side*, but she's just as good, if not better, in *Infamous*.

BEST SCENE
Sandra and Jones argue over the direction he's taking his supposed "non-fiction" novel.

BEST LINE
"You shouldn't be doing what you're doing!"

FUN FACTS

Sandra won the 2006 Hollywood Film Festival award for Best Supporting Actress for this film.

Infamous reunited Sandra with her *Speed* co-star Jeff Daniels.

Samantha Morton was originally cast as Harper Lee.

The film's original title alternated between *Have You Heard?* and *Every Word is True*.

Sandra did not personally meet Harper Lee, but she did extensive research, including listening to her voice in audio clips and studying her handwriting on microfiche at the New York Public Library.

PREMONITION (2007)

FILM FACTS

DISTRIBUTOR: MGM
PRODUCTION COMPANY: Hyde Park Entertainment
RELEASE DATE: March 16, 2007

DIRECTOR: Mennan Yapo
WRITER: Bill Kelly
PRODUCERS: Ashok Amritaj, Jennifer Gibgot, Jon Jashni, Sunil Perkash, Adam Shankman
ALSO STARRING: Julian McMahon, Nia Long, Kate Nelligan, Jude Ciccolella, Amber Valletta

REVIEW

Sandra's career has had its ups and downs from the very beginning, but if she took two steps forward with *Crash* in 2005 and *Infamous* in 2006, she took a major step back in 2007 with the dreadful *Premonition*, easily one of the worst and most ridiculous movies she's ever participated in. What was she thinking when she signed on for this one? There are a few decent moments in *Premonition*, including a conclusion that thankfully doesn't give us the predictable feel-good ending, but mostly this is a laughable, absurd thriller that does nobody involved any favors.

Apparently Sandra was looking for something scary to do, something that called back to the classic work of Alfred Hitchcock. She didn't want to do a horror film necessarily, but more of a psychological thriller. She said she was looking at a lot of projects in this genre, but as soon as she started flipping through the *Premonition* script, she was certain this was the one she wanted to make. It's a shame because of all the genres Sandra has done really well, she has yet to make a successful "scary" movie. It's a shame, too, because with a better script and director, *Premonition* could have at least been serviceable entertainment. The idea is sort of intriguing. But it needed a more talented group behind the scenes. In the end, Sandra is left with not much to work with here.

The film opens with Sandra going through the daily motions. She plays Linda, a mom of two. She drives her kids to school, takes a jog, does the laundry. It's just like any other day. Then the doorbell rings, and she finds a police officer standing outside. "Your husband's been in an accident," he says. "He died at the scene." She spends the rest of the day in mourning, like any person would do. Her mother comes to visit that night, and tells her she needs to start thinking about funeral arrangements. "I'm not ready for that yet, Mom," she says. She wakes up the next day, comes downstairs, and, lo and behold, her husband Jim (a bored looking Julian McMahon) is alive and well! Huh? What happened? She assumes yesterday was all a dream. But then she wakes up the *next* morning to find that her husband's dead again, and it's time to attend the funeral. What? It turns out that Linda is waking up on a different random day of a seven-day week. Back and forth, over on this day and then over on that one. Will she be able to save her husband's life?

This film goes wrong in so many ways. Its biggest problem is that it's boring. Never do we really care about her husband, or if she'll save him, or if she even wants to save him. His character is such a dullard it doesn't even affect the viewer to a great extent when he's mutilated in the big explosive ending. We never get to really know him, aside from the fact that he's a decent father but has been cheating on Linda with another woman. "If I let Jim die, is that the same thing as killing him?" Linda says in one of the film's few good moments, a line that also ended the ridiculous trailer released at the end of 2006. How much more interesting would that ending have been? If she knew her husband's death was coming, and she sat back and did nothing to stop it? The ending of the movie is not a happily ever after by any means, but that would have been truly unexpected.

The film has so many funny moments that it almost works as a comedy. The first hilarious moment occurs when Linda is at the church to attend her husband's funeral, when she has a momentary freak-out and runs over to the hearse, demanding she see her husband's corpse. The two pallbearers accidentally drop the casket, allowing her husband's severed head to go bouncing down the sidewalk. Sandra's over-the-top theatrics make the scene funnier, and the complete non-reaction by Kate Nelligan (who plays her mother, Joanne) only adds to the fun. Let's see, what else. There's Linda's oldest daughter running through the house and crashing through fake, unmistakable CGI glass. Or Linda telling her husband, on the last night he's alive: "We're running out of time!" Or Linda frantically writing out the days of the week on paper, trying to formulate in her head which days she's lived through, and which ones she has yet to see. She surmises that Jim dies on Wednesday! So she writes Jim Dies, then puts three big lines underneath, to show that this is an important date! There are so many absurd moments in *Premonition* that it's hard to keep track of them all.

The fault lies in the screenplay by Bill Kelly, which thinks it's clever but has enough plot holes to run a steamroller through. (The most obvious of which is that on the day Linda finds out her husband has died, her oldest daughter has no cuts on her face, even though the incident where she crashes through the glass has already happened.) It also lies in the pedestrian, clichéd direction of a German director named Mennan Yapo, who made one movie before *Premonition*, and zero since. He doesn't have the visual style, or the eye for detail, needed for the film's intricate story. Imagine what someone like Darren Aronofsky or David Fincher could have done with this material.

Worst of all is that Yapo directs Sandra to one of her misguided performances ever. It's the best and worst element of the movie: Sandra is in nearly every shot of the entire 96-minute movie, a designation not given since probably *The Net*, in 1995 (a much better Sandra thriller), and yet she looks completely lost here, and not in a good way. She claims in one of the behind-the-scenes interviews that *Premonition* was not her favorite acting experience, because as filming went on she became more and more confused as to where her character was emotionally in each scene she filmed. Think about it. The character wakes up on seven different days throughout the film, and Yapo shot the movie out of sequence. So Sandra, who probably worked every day of the film's forty-five-day shoot, had to every morning piece together where her character was on that day, what she knew, and what she didn't know. It had to be exhausting; two months of that must have been torture. What did Yapo say when Sandra shouted in annoyance that she was losing her mind? "It's good! It's the character!" Apparently Yapo's directing strategy was to make Sandra the person go insane, to make the character on screen look like *she's* going insane. Actually, Sandra doesn't look insane at all in the movie. Aside from a couple of effective moments—Linda walking downstairs to see everyone dressed for the funeral and telling her mom, "Something is really, really wrong"—she typically looks vaguely distant, like she's thinking about when she'll be done filming the damn movie so she can go home.

Sandra's exciting on screen when she's fired up to be there, appearing in a story that moves her, and playing a character that challenges her—think *The Blind Side* or *Gravity*—but unfortunately *Premonition* includes one of Sandra's weakest characters and dramatic performances of her career post-*Speed*.

BEST SCENE
Sandra witnesses her husband's explosive demise.

BEST LINE

"Something is really fucked up about this situation!"

FUN FACTS

It was Sandra's idea to have Linda pregnant in the final scene of the film.

This was not a remake of the 2004 Japanese horror film of the same name.

The original script was to have Linda save Jim, but that seemed too "Hollywood," so they ended up making it more dark.

Despite the negative reviews, *Premonition* was a mild box office success, making $84 million worldwide on a budget of only $20 million.

Although they play mother and daughter in this movie, Kate Nelligan is only thirteen years older than Sandra.

Sandra said she wanted to do a Hitchcock-ian film. There actually was an episode of *Alfred Hitchcock Presents* called "Premonition," starring John Forsythe and Cloris Leachman.

THE PROPOSAL (2009)

FILM FACTS

DISTRIBUTOR: Touchstone Pictures
PRODUCTION COMPANY: Mandeville Films
RELEASE DATE: June 19, 2009

DIRECTOR: Anne Fletcher
WRITER: Peter Chiarelli
PRODUCERS: David Hoberman, Todd Lieberman
ALSO STARRING: Ryan Reynolds, Mary Steenburgen, Betty White,
Craig T. Nelson, Malin Akerman

REVIEW

And then there was 2009. For fans all around the world, this truly was the year of Sandra. After disappearing from cinema screens for nearly two and a half years, she returned with not one, not two, but *three* feature films in 2009, all released within just five short months of each other. Now there have been many actors who have had three (or more) movies released in one given year (remember Natalie Portman's epic run of six films between *Black Swan* and *Thor*?). There have even been actors who have made multiple movies in a given year and went on to win an Academy Award for one of them (think Jennifer

Lawrence in 2012, with *The Hunger Games*, *House at the End of the Street*, and *Silver Linings Playbook*).

But not even Lawrence could replicate all the accolades and major milestones of what Sandra did in 2009. Her first film of the year, *The Proposal*, released in June, went on to make $163 million nationwide, becoming one of the smash hit comedies of the summer, and earned Sandra a Golden Globe nomination for Best Actress in a Comedy. *All About Steve*, released in September, went on to only make $33 million (the same amount *The Proposal* made in its opening weekend) and earn her the Razzie Award for Worst Actress. Don't worry, though—one more little film came out in November. *The Blind Side* went on to make a whopping $256 million nationwide, and win for Sandra the Critic's Choice award, Golden Globe award, Screen Actors Guild award, and Academy Award. Let's just say Sandra had a busy year.

But it all started with *The Proposal*, which is easily her funniest, most enjoyable romantic comedy since *While You Were Sleeping*. She stars as Margaret Tate, a respected and powerful book editor in New York who learns that she's about to be deported back to Canada for at least a year for having an expired VISA. She has no intention of leaving, though, so she blackmails her longtime assistant Andrew (Ryan Reynolds) to marry her, or he'll be on the street looking for a new job, and his dreams of being a published author will be dead. But when it's suspected that they might be committing fraud, they are forced to go up to Andrew's family home for the weekend to take part in the ninetieth birthday celebration of Gammy (a delightful Betty White), and try to learn as much about each other as they can before their big interview on Monday. Of course, Andrew already knows everything there is to know about her, being her secretary morning to night, sometimes seven days a week, for three years running, while she knows next to nothing about him. And of course, throughout the weekend, they just might find themselves falling in love— for real.

The Proposal is not an especially original movie. You pretty much know where it's going once its premise is established, and the arc of Sandra's character is about as predictable as it gets. The film is directed by Anne Fletcher, who is not exactly known for making great works of art— she makes fun popcorn movies, and that's exactly what *The Proposal* is. It's the kind of movie you go to in the summer with your friends, have a few good laughs, and move on with your night. It's not something you necessarily think about for long stretches afterward. But does it make you laugh? Yes. Is there chemistry between the two leads? Double yes. Does it feature one of Sandra's better performances? Absolutely!

While in the 2000s Sandra turned in mediocre performances in equally mediocre films like *Murder by Numbers*, *Divine Secrets of the Ya-Ya Sisterhood*, and *Premonition*, *The Proposal* is Sandra at her comedic best. Here is a character who has been alone most of her life, and who has had to work her way to the top through sweat, blood, and tears over three decades. She has no semblance of a family life, and no semblance of a life, period. In the beginning of the film, she is essentially the younger stepsister of Meryl

Streep in *The Devil Wears Prada*, with her tight black suit and no-nonsense ponytail, and a calm, composed way of firing people. She's not the Sandra we know and love in the beginning. But when she arrives at Andrew's parents' house, everything changes. She slowly starts to come out of her shell, all the way to the end when she discovers she might have the capacity to feel real emotion, and give all her love to someone. She is in complete control of this character from the first scene, and it's one of her most inspired and likable performances.

Anne Fletcher, who also directed *27 Dresses* and *The Guilt Trip*, is the kind of director who mostly stays out of the way of her actors, and allows the story to unfold as naturally as possible. Her work is never on the subtle side, but one thing she does really well is casting (yes, even *27 Dresses*, which features Katherine Heigl's best lead performance in a movie). *The Proposal* benefits from Sandra's performance, but it's also guided along by a terrific supporting cast. Reynolds is almost too good looking for his role, but their relationship is very believable, and he rightly underplays his growing affection for his boss. They are really cute together, and despite their age difference (twelve years in real life), you can accept their attraction to each other, and that he would come to her at the end and say, "Marry me, because I want to date you." Malin Akerman, Mary Steenburgen, Craig T. Nelson, and especially Denis O'Hare are very fine in underwritten roles. And then there's White, whose last big career renaissance started with the release of *The Proposal*. Playing a woman on the verge of ninety, she's got as much spunk as a teenager.

Her reactions are priceless, all throughout the movie, and it's especially fun to see her and Sandra, two of our most gifted comediennes, play off each other.

In terms of the comedy, I found in watching *The Proposal* again for the first time since 2009 that the more subtle moments get laughs and the big scenes meant for uproarious laughter haven't held up as well. Take for example the much discussed and promoted scene where the two leads bump into each other naked. While this is still a funny moment, the build-up to it is so contrived in its construction that it drains some of the fun away. The lap dance scene never really worked, and Margaret dancing and chanting in the forest still doesn't ring true to me. I prefer the more subtle jokes, like Andrew sending out IM messages about his boss to everyone in the office, White saying, "she comes with a lot of baggage!" and Margaret trying to fall asleep with the Alaskan sun streaming in through the window.

In terms of the drama, the movie is way better than it has any right to be, and this is mostly due to Sandra's performance. The scene when Margaret jumps into the boat and steers out to open waters, screaming about how she forgot what it was like to have a family, is a great moment. In the hands of a lesser actress, this scene might have come across as sentimental, but Sandra sells it. The wedding scene toward the end, where Margaret faces the crowd and finally reveals the truth, is also effective. She is subtle in this scene, never going over-the-top. And then there's the finale back in the New York office. This key moment, by all accounts, shouldn't work nearly as well as it does (especially since it was a new ending written and shot long after production had already wrapped). But the way Sandra plays this scene is beautifully subtle. Another actress could have thrown herself at Reynolds, with the music swelling, as she kissed him and said, "I love you, I love you!" Instead she just stands there for most of the scene, her eyes slowly welling with tears, as she gives him reasons why he shouldn't be with her. But when he keeps pressing, with nowhere for her to go, she says, after a long, powerful beat, "I'm scared." The woman who ruled the world in the first scene, in the end is terrified of finally opening up her emotional side. Of any scene in *The Proposal*, this scene is the most touching, and shows Sandra at the height of her dramatic power.

Like *The Blind Side*, Sandra took a long time to commit to *The Proposal*. If you remember, back in the early 2000s, she claimed that *Two Weeks Notice*, the pleasant but unremarkable movie she made with Hugh Grant, would be her last romantic comedy. She was so committed to this idea that for months she refused to even look at the script. She said no, I'm done with this genre, no more. The producer and director, and her agents no doubt, begged her just to read it, so she could officially pass. So of course Sandra read it, and loved it, and happily accepted. It is one of the oddities of her films released in 2009 that the two movies she said no to for months ultimately made hundreds of millions and won her tons of awards—but the one she committed to early on, and even produced through her production company Fortis Films, was the bomb that netted her the Razzie. Go figure. We can all be thankful that people pushed Sandra into committing to *The Proposal* and *The Blind Side*, because they made for two of her best films and biggest hits. Is *The Proposal* a great movie? No. But it gives Sandra one of her richest performances to date.

BEST SCENE
Sandra, in the end, gets her real proposal.

BEST LINE
"You can't fight a love like ours! So… are we good?"

FUN FACTS

Julia Roberts was the first choice to play Margaret, but reportedly refused to take a pay cut, so Sandra took over the role.

Betty White almost turned down her role because filming required her to spend ten weeks away from her golden retriever.

The film was remade in 2012 as a Malayalam-language Indian film, *My Boss*.

Sandra received a Golden Globe nomination for Best Actress in a Comedy/Musical, her first nomination in this category since *Miss Congeniality*.

In this film, Sandra plays a Canadian who wants to marry her American assistant. In real life, Reynolds is from Canada and Sandra is American.

The Proposal grossed $317 million worldwide, becoming the highest grossing romantic comedy of 2009, and one of Sandra's biggest hits to date.

ALL ABOUT STEVE (2009)

FILM FACTS

DISTRIBUTOR: Fox 2000 Pictures
PRODUCTION COMPANY: Fortis Films
RELEASE DATE: September 4, 2009

DIRECTOR: Phil Traill
WRITER: Kim Barker
PRODUCERS: Sandra Bullock, Mary McLaglen
ALSO STARRING: Bradley Cooper, Thomas Haden Church, Ken Jeong, DJ Qualls, Beth Grant

REVIEW

"To my husband, there's no surprise that my work got better when I met you, because I never knew what it felt like for someone to have my back. So thank you." – Sandra receiving her Golden Globe for *The Blind Side*.

In one of her many touching speeches of the 2010 awards season, Sandra ended her concise speech at the Golden Globes with two lies: one we didn't know yet, and one we already knew. The one we didn't know was that in March it turned out that Sandra's husband Jesse James had been cheating on her with multiple women for many months, maybe even years, and did in fact *not* have her back. The one we already knew? While Sandra again proved her comedy chops in the blockbuster hit *The Proposal*, and stretched as a dramatic actress in her Oscar-winning role in *The Blind Side*, not all of her work necessarily got better after she met James. She did make *Miss Congeniality 2*. And *Premonition*. And, dear God, *All About Steve*.

Yes, we have arrived to the big, fat golden turkey of Sandra's career. She's made some bad movies, for sure—but nothing she has made comes close to the horrors of *All About Steve*, a so-called "comedy" that sat on the shelf for more than two years. The film ultimately came out with little fanfare and promotion on Labor Day weekend, until it quickly and quietly disappeared into oblivion. It doesn't help that there are almost zero laughs in the film's entire running time, or that the funniest thing about it is that lame photo-shopped DVD cover. What makes *All About Steve* particularly fascinating is that it's a train-wreck that came out sandwiched between two of the biggest smash hits of her career, and one that, when Sandra received her first Oscar, came back to haunt her… when she received Worst Actress at the Razzies the very night before!

2009 was easily the most eventful, most fascinating year of Sandra's career, with the win for both the Oscar and the Razzie in early 2010 capping off a very strange and exciting time. So did Sandra deserve the Razzie for *All About Steve*? She didn't win for lack of trying. When she picked up the award the night before the Oscars, she doubted that most of the voting body had even seen *All About Steve*, so she brought a truck of DVDs to ensure that each member would go home and watch it—and as she said in her hilarious speech, *really* watch it — and that everyone would see what she was trying to do. If you actively watch *All About Steve*, it's clear that Sandra is *not* phoning in a performance. Unlike, say, *Premonition*, she is actually trying in *All About Steve*. Unfortunately, in this case, just because she tries to create a unique character and do something different, it doesn't necessarily mean that what appears on the screen is any good. And in the case of *All About Steve*, almost nothing works, including Sandra's manic, oddball performance.

I took a friend of mine to an empty Van Nuys movie theater on the Sunday of Labor Day weekend to see Sandra's newest effort. The second half of 2009 was magical for a Sandra fan. While two years passed after *Premonition* with nothing, we were suddenly inundated with three Sandra movies within five months. *The Proposal* delightfully surprised me, and by September some Oscar buzz had already started building for *The Blind Side*. I knew going into *All About Steve* that the reviews were bad, and that the word of mouth was even worse, but I didn't care. If *The Proposal* was the appetizer and *The Blind Side* was the main course, I figured *All About Steve* would be the cheese snack in the middle, something light and forgettable. Unfortunately I knew only ten minutes into *All About Steve* that this was going to be one of her rougher movies. And then it only got worse.

The film tells of Mary Horowitz (Sandra), an eccentric crossword puzzle maker who lives at home and has no friends or romantic prospects. Her parents (played by Howard Hesseman and Beth Grant, the latter having now

---

174

co-starred with Sandra in three other films, including *Speed*) set her up on a blind date with a handsome cameraman Steve (Bradley Cooper, who shot his part in the film prior to *The Hangover*). But before he's even able to drive the car down the street, she straddles him, kisses him, tries to have sex with him. He's into it at first, but then she keeps talking and talking and talking. He gets a call about a job and takes off, glad he doesn't have to spend another minute with her. But when Mary is let go from her job, after creating a crossword puzzle dedicated to Steve and only Steve, she takes it as a sign that she's supposed to be with him. So, with her crazy red boots and trusty umbrella in tow, she sets off on a cross-country journey to find Steve, the man she believes she's meant to be with. Will they meet again? Will they end up together? Do we care?

Phil Traill, who made his feature directorial debut with *All About Steve*, sprinkles the film with many good comedic actors, including Thomas Haden Church (who admits in the DVD behind-the-scenes that he had to be coaxed into signing on for this one), Ken Jeong, DJ Qualls, Holmes Osborne, and Keith David, among others, but the screenplay by Kim Barker leaves the director, and the cast, little to work with. The central problem with the film is that we never have any rooting interest for Mary to find Steve, or achieve her dreams, or, well, *anything*. She's a kook that Sandra tries her best to bring to life, but she's never rooted in any reality we can get behind. As much as I love Sandra, she seems ten years too old for this part, with Cooper seeming way too young for her here (in real life, they are eleven years apart). Of course, the age difference in *The*

Proposal worked because she was the boss and Ryan Reynolds was the assistant—and the two actors actually had chemistry. Sandra and Cooper feel more like older sister and younger brother than love interests, so there's never anything to get behind in terms of their relationship.

So when that all goes, what are you left with? If nothing else, there was an opportunity here to lampoon newsmagazine programs. But those scenes fall flat, too. Church is so naturally funny that it's astonishing he doesn't get a single laugh here, playing a vain on-camera news reporter. (In fact, the only laughs in all of *All About Steve* come from Church, not in the film, but on the DVD commentary, which is way more fun than the movie itself.) Jeong, who usually plays the strangest character in each of his films, plays the straight man in this, to dull results. And Cooper just looks lost the whole time, like he's stumbled onto set and doesn't know what movie he's in. There are a few chuckles when Jeong's character finally explodes and goes off on the other two, but at this point in the movie, we've lost all interest.

There's Mary's journey toward Steve, which is full of road-stops and new friends and tornados and long falls, but none of this material works, either. Are we supposed to be laughing when Mary and her two new buddies approach an oncoming tornado and run for the nearest shelter? What is this scene supposed to do, exactly? The effect looks great, but not a single laugh is even attempted in this scene. So what's the point? And all the little obstacles Mary hits on her way to Steve just come off like padding to get the movie to ninety minutes, rather than authentic moments

176

that a real person in her situation might encounter. Of course, none of this would matter if you were laughing. But you watch the film stupefied how anyone thought this would have made a good movie, let alone a watchable one. Most head-scratching of all is that not only did Sandra play the lead, but she produced the film, too. Maybe the script read better in the beginning? Maybe they made so many changes that some of the better ideas from early drafts got lost in the shuffle? Maybe Sandra just really needed a paycheck?

I was mortified by this movie in September 2009 but I came to it again, in 2014, with an open mind. Maybe five years later it would come off more as a funky, offbeat road comedy, and not be the disaster I believed it to be at that first viewing. I thought after suffering through *Miss Congeniality 2* and *Premonition* again, in recent months, this one might actually come off better than I remembered. But nope—nothing has improved. In fact, I even came to like it less. Because no matter how insipid and clunky and longwinded the first seventy-five percent of the movie is, nothing prepares you for the finale of *All About Steve*.

It's like something out of movie hell, the kind that can never be erased from your mind. A group of deaf children fall into a mine, and all but one are rescued. Steve, of course, is on the scene filming, and Mary appears, so excited to see him again that she runs toward him, doesn't see the hole, and falls to the bottom of the mine. When she crawls out of the water that broke her fall, she discovers a little deaf girl who she needs to save, and who she apparently needs to spill all her life lessons to. This scene might have read funny on the page in an early draft, but it is positively deadly on the screen—and it goes on forever. After an hour and ten minutes of non-comedy, the movie suddenly tries to be sincere, and even profound, and fails miserably. Since Mary has no chance with Steve, there's nowhere for the writer Barker to go, except try to prove to audiences everywhere that nut-balls like Mary Horowitz should be admired, not shunned, and should be waved around in the air like heroes. The last twenty minutes of *All About Steve* are so mind-numbingly absurd that it almost works as so-bad-it's-good cinema. Almost.

I can see an alien race stumbling onto a pile of DVDs that would give them information about what the human race was like at the turn of the twenty-first century, with the first disc they put for a spin in the player being *All About Steve*. They just might fly right back to where they came from. *All About Steve* is the most embarrassing movie of Sandra's career—and that's a statement coming from a super fan. When I met Sandra in Santa Barbara in February 2010, I told her I loved all her movies. "Have you *seen* all my movies?" she quipped. "Well, *All About Steve* was pretty rough," I could have said—but I didn't want to be rude. She had such a great year in 2009 that this film seemed to only serve one purpose: to give her one more award (not the positive kind) to place on her mantle. She was the biggest movie star of that year, and even a colossal mess like *All About Steve* wasn't going to change that; she's had such a long career that one bad movie, especially one sandwiched between two good ones, won't change a thing. Thank God for *The Blind Side*, and thank God for her

Oscar, because we'll likely never see a movie like *All About Steve* for the rest of Sandra's career. I mean, hopefully, right? *Right?*

BEST SCENE
When the movie ends.

BEST LINE
"I will eat you like a mountain lion."

FUN FACTS

All About Steve was nominated for five Razzie awards, including Worst Picture, and won two: Worst Actress for Sandra, and Worst Screen Couple, for Sandra and Cooper.

The film grossed $33 million at the nationwide box office, far less than her other two 2009 releases.

To date, the last film Sandra has produced through her production company, Fortis Films.

Shot in the summer of 2007, but not released until September 2009.

When Mary is soaking in the tub, the song in the background is sung by Helga Bullock, Sandra's mother.

THE BLIND SIDE (2009)

FILM FACTS

DISTRIBUTOR: Warner Bros.
PRODUCTION COMPANY: Zucker/Netter Productions
RELEASE DATE: November 20, 2009

DIRECTOR: John Lee Hancock
WRITER: John Lee Hancock (based on the book, *The Blind Side: Evolution of a Game*, by Michael Lewis)
PRODUCERS: Broderick Johnson, Andrew A. Kosove, Gil Netter
ALSO STARRING: Quinton Aaron, Tim McGraw, Jae Head, Lily Collins, Kathy Bates

REVIEW

I remember that Sunday night like it was last week. All my life I had loved the Academy Awards, and all my life I had loved Sandra, and suddenly, unexpectedly, two of my favorite things lined up into one amazing event. As much as I love Sandra, and as much I always knew she had better work in her, I had my doubts that Sandra would ever even be *nominated* for an Oscar, let alone win one. *Crash* and *Infamous* showed that with a great script and director, she absolutely could be in contention, but after practically suffocating in movies like *Premonition* and *All About Steve*, I wasn't sure if the stars would ever align, not just for Sandra to finally be taken seriously, but for her to give a performance so beloved that she'd be recognized by her peers. Early 2010 was such a surreal time for Sandra fans, as we watched her collect trophy after trophy, kiss Meryl Streep at the Critic's Choice Awards, bow in front of Warren Beatty at the Screen Actors Guild Awards, and arrive to the Oscars on Sunday, March 7th, as the frontrunner for Best Actress. After a long, not very exciting show, Sandra's moment finally arrived.

When Oprah Winfrey and Forest Whitaker, among others, took to the stage, I turned to my friend Katie Bode and said, "Someone needs to be filming me. I'm going to freak out if she wins." So when Sean Penn stumbled up to the microphone, the envelope in his hand, I started pacing the room—and the camera started rolling. Even as the seconds ticked down to the big reveal, I wasn't sure if Sandra's name would be called, but I also felt like, if she ever had a shot at winning, this was her year. Would Sandra have won the year before if she had been up against Kate Winslet for *The Reader*? No way. Would she have beaten Natalie Portman for *Black Swan* a year later? Probably not. The only other real Best Actress contender of 2009 was Meryl Streep, in *Julie & Julia*. But even though she's great in that film, and hadn't won an Oscar since the early '80s, she's only in half the movie. Penn opened the envelope and read, "And the winner is… Sandra Bullock, in *The Blind Side*." I started jumping, screaming, rolling around on the floor. I even had to excuse myself from the room for a moment, I was so excited. Think I'm making this up?

Search "Sandra Bullock Oscar Freakout" on Youtube. As much as it looks like I'm faking my reaction, it really was one hundred percent real, as I explained in an interview I did for *Inside Edition* (also online).

When I think of *The Blind Side* now, it's hard to separate the movie from awards season, and especially my crazy Oscar reaction video that received nearly 100,000 hits and comments like "this guy need to be blind sided by a bus" (my personal favorite), so it was a joy, really, to revisit the film nearly five years since its release to see if my initial reaction had changed at all. When I saw *The Blind Side* opening night in November 2009, I walked out satisfied but unmoved. I'll never forget the first words I said to my friend Katie when we walked out of the theater: "Sandra was good but she's not gonna be nominated." So here I am, one of her biggest fans, and I didn't even think she would receive a nomination, despite the fact she went on to win every award known to man that season. Is Sandra's performance as Leigh Ann Tuohy in *The Blind Side* on par with, say, Helen Mirren's in *The Queen*, or Meryl Streep's in *The Iron Lady*? Of course not.

But what I missed the first time while I watched *The Blind Side* was the smart subtle choices Sandra makes throughout the movie. The first time I kept waiting for that big "Oscar" scene, where she would start crying and scream with joy toward the ceiling about how much she loves her new adopted son. Sandra only goes big, so to speak, in a couple of scenes, like when she yells at the gang members. Most of her powerful moments, though, take place when she's quiet, when you just watch her thinking. At the time even I wasn't sure if Sandra's performance in *The Blind Side* was worthy of the Academy Award, but when I look at the film now, away from all the hype and hoopla of awards season, I see that she was absolutely the best choice to win. She is terrific in this movie.

Aside from a third act conflict that slows the pacing down a bit, *The Blind Side* works on many levels, as a football movie, a family drama, a rags-to-riches story, and a journey toward self-discovery, both for Leigh Anne and for Michael Oher (Quinton Aaron). The film is based on a true story, about a rich white Christian family of four who take in a poor black seventeen-year-old named Michael, whose GPA never reaches above 1.0 and who's been in and out of foster care his whole life. After he becomes more comfortable in his new family unit, he tries out for football and becomes the star player, ultimately earning scholarships to any college of his choosing; a few years later he became offensive lineman for the Baltimore Ravens of the NFL. It's one of those stories you wouldn't believe if it were fiction. It's truly inspiring, and writer/director John Lee Hancock (*Saving Mr. Banks*, *The Rookie*) is smart in letting the events unfold in a mostly traditional way, without too many directorial flourishes that could have gotten in the way of the narrative.

What I love most about *The Blind Side* is the family dynamic the director and actors manage to create. Sandra told Charlie Rose, in a revealing interview in early 2010, that she struggled in finding a way into the character of Leigh Anne the first day of filming, but that once the family unit arrived on set, everything started to click. The four

183

actors play off each other really well, and never in a way that seems forced. Tim McGraw may not be the best actor in the world, but he comes off as very natural here, especially in his quieter scenes with Sandra. I love the way he accepts Leigh Anne the way she is and allows her to take control when he knows there's no stopping her. The kids are adorable, Jae Head as S.J. and Lily Collins as Collins. Head is the movie's prime comic relief; it's amazing how funny and refreshingly authentic he is throughout, never coming off as a dumb movie kid. Collins, the older and pretty teenage sister, easily could've been the cliché smart-mouth of the family clan, but instead is warm and genuine throughout. It doesn't seem like Quinton Aaron, as Michael, would fit in with these people, but he does, almost from the beginning—and with each scene that passes, we want him to be included without judgment in this family.

But more than anything, this film gave Sandra the chance to finally stretch her acting muscles on a large-scale capacity. While she did terrific dramatic work in *Crash* and *Infamous*, her screen-time in those movies is limited. In *The Blind Side*, she's the star, and she never has one false move. I love her introduction in the movie, her pushing past teenagers, yapping away on a cell phone, trying to get to a seat for her daughter's volleyball game. We know in her very first shot the kind of woman we're about to meet. She's loud, pushy, speaks her mind—and, as her husband attests to a lot throughout the movie, always gets her way. Of course there's the look, with the long blonde hair, glossy make-up, affluent conservative wardrobes. But deep down she's the kind of woman who wants to do the right thing, so when she comes across Michael shivering in the cold, she doesn't let ten seconds pass before she decides to take him home. Sandra and Aaron work well off each other, especially as he grows more tender and affectionate toward her. Of course it didn't hurt that while filming this movie, Sandra in real life was getting close to adopting a baby boy of her own, enabling her to truly relate to this story and character. (In her Oscar speech, she even says, "what this film is about for me are the moms who take care of the children and the babies no matter where they come from.")

Some may look at her "bigger" moments in the movie as her best, like when she tells off the woman at the DMV, or when she schools Michael on the football field about how to treat his teammates like a family. I, however, also love the subtle moments, like when she asks Michael if he'd like to be a part of the family, and has to excuse herself from the table when her eyes start welling up with tears, or the way she looks at him when he says he's never even had a bed before. Sandra could have overplayed some of these quieter moments, but she never does. She becomes this character, through and through. She never tries to go for that emotional close-up, and she never lets any "Sandra Bullock-isms" seep into the performance. Part of what makes her performances in *Crash* and *Infamous* so startling is that she really does lose herself, of everything we know about her. She disappears into Leigh Anne from the very beginning, and, while she manages to be funny and vulnerable and caring, qualities she exudes both in other films and as a human being, they are all essential to the character, and the arc she gets to play over the course of this very fine film.

The Blind Side opened on November 20, 2009, up against *Twilight: New Moon*, which, of course, enjoyed one of the biggest opening weekends ever. Even Sandra herself questioned the decision to open *The Blind Side* against a juggernaut like the *Twilight* sequel. Of course the choice turned out to be an inspired one, given that *The Blind Side* opened with $35 million, went up in profit the second weekend, and stepped ahead of *New Moon* in the third weekend to become the nation's number one movie. Why the love? Everyone enjoys a good sports movie; mix in a fascinating true life story and Sandra, at the top of her craft, and a hit you are practically guaranteed. The movie is notable for being the first to cross the $200 million-dollar mark at the box office having only one actress's name above the title. Topping out at $256 million nationwide, *The Blind Side* became one of the most profitable films in recent history, proving that Sandra was not just still America's sweetheart, but also one of a few select actors who can bring in audiences of all ages.

2009 was Sandra's banner year at the movies, and even though the three films she made are definitely inconsistent in terms of quality, each one demonstrated the different kinds of women Sandra's capable of playing. In *The Proposal*, she plays a powerful book editor who prefers to be alone. In *All About Steve*, she plays a crazy stalker loner who just wants to be accepted. And in *The Blind Side*, she plays a devout Christian wife and mother of two who takes a kid in need off the street and ends up changing her family's life forever. These three roles couldn't be any more different from each other, and they did a great job that year in showing the kind of range she has, and how adept she is at both comedy and drama.

But as much fun as *The Proposal* is, and how perfectly dreadful *All About Steve* turned out to be, it's *The Blind Side* that marked the great turning point in Sandra's career. For fifteen years, between *Speed* and *The Blind Side*, I kept lamenting how Sandra continued to pick bad scripts and mediocre directors. She was rarely stepping out of her comfort zone, or taking on material that might challenge her. Of course that all changed after *The Blind Side*, because the following year Sandra signed on for *Extremely Loud & Incredibly Close*, directed by thrice-Oscar-nominated Stephen Daldry, and *Gravity*, directed by the great Alfonso Cuaron. Would Sandra have been considered for *Gravity*, if it hadn't have been for *The Blind Side*? Not likely. As ridiculous as it sounds, winning an Academy Award raises your pedigree in Hollywood, especially for someone like Sandra, who might not have been thought of for more weighty dramatic roles in the past. Many probably wouldn't have immediately thought of Sandra for the role in *The Blind Side*, and thankfully John Lee Hancock did. With this beloved film, Sandra finally got to show what she could do. Today? There's no stopping her.

BEST SCENE
Sandra explains to Michael how playing football is about protecting the family.

―――

BEST LINE

"If you so much as set foot downtown, you will be sorry. I'm in a prayer group with the D.A., I'm a member of the NRA, and I'm always packing."

FUN FACTS

For this film, Sandra won the Academy Award, Screen Actors Guild Award, Golden Globe, and Critic's Choice Award.

The Blind Side was nominated for Best Picture at the Academy Awards. It lost to *The Hurt Locker*.

This film is the highest grossing sports drama of all time.

This is the first movie to gross more than $200 million that features a sole actress's name above the title.

When Quinton Aaron auditioned for the film, he was working as a security guard.

Julia Roberts was offered the role of Leigh Anne Touhy, but turned it down. She also turned down the role of Margaret Tate in *The Proposal*. Sandra should be happy Roberts likes to say no to things.

Sandra has strong ties to the south. Her father was from Alabama, and she was born and raised in Virginia, and attended college in North Carolina.

Sandra took a pay cut to make the film and agreed to a percentage of the profits, which turned out to be a *very* smart move on her part.

EXTREMELY LOUD & INCREDIBLE CLOSE (2011)

FILM FACTS

DISTRIBUTOR: Warner Bros.
PRODUCTION COMPANY: Scott Rudin Productions
RELEASE DATE: December 25, 2011

DIRECTOR: Stephen Daldry
WRITER: Eric Roth (based on the novel by Jonathan Safran Foer)
PRODUCER: Scott Rudin
ALSO STARRING: Tom Hanks, Thomas Horn, Jeffrey Wright, Viola
Davis, John Goodman, Max von Sydow

REVIEW

After winning the Academy Award for *The Blind Side* in
March 2010, Sandra was faced with the ultimate question:
what's next? While she navigated the awards circuit that
spring, she said she wasn't even looking at scripts, and after
the whole Jesse James debacle went down, Sandra
disappeared from public life for about three months. When
she re-emerged that summer at the MTV Movie Awards to
accept her Generation Award (where a terrific two-minute
montage of her film work was screened), she said that she

loves what she does, and that she wasn't going anywhere. I remember rumors floating around that time that she was even considering quitting the film business, but such, thankfully, was not the case.

While Sandra laid low for the rest of 2010, she re-emerged in 2011 on the sets of not one but two films, both that would challenge her in ways we never could have expected. When she won her Oscar, what I hoped, more than anything, was that truly talented directors would finally see Sandra as more than "America's Sweetheart" or the "Romantic Comedy Queen" and take her seriously as an actress, and potentially give her some meaty roles. On February 25, 2011, two days before she handed Colin Firth his Oscar for *The King's Speech*, Sandra began production on her first film post-*The Blind Side*, post-Jesse, post the most insane time in her public life that will (likely) ever be. For the first time, Sandra was working with a stellar group of talent that included acclaimed director Stephen Daldry (*The Hours*, *The Reader*), screenwriter Eric Roth (*Forrest Gump*), the powerhouse producer Scott Rudin (*No Country for Old Men*, *True Grit*), and Mr. Tom Hanks—all in a film based on a celebrated novel. Slam dunk, right? *Extremely Loud & Incredibly Close*, released at the end of 2011, would go on to receive big praise, and even be nominated for Best Picture at the Academy Awards—but the film, unfortunately, is a mess, and despite some good scenes, including two with Sandra, the film never finds the right tone.

Based on the 2005 novel by Jonathan Safran Foer, *Extremely Loud & Incredibly Close* tells the story of Oskar Schell (newcomer Thomas Horn), a thoughtful, autistic nine-year-old whose best friend in the world—his dad (Hanks)—dies unexpectedly in the World Trade Center attacks. A year later, he goes into his closet, which his mom Linda (Sandra) still hasn't touched. He accidentally breaks an urn that encases an envelope that says BLACK, with a small key inside. He thinks that finding the recipient to the key might bring him more answers about his father, so he runs around New York City and talks to anyone with the last name of Black. Along the way, he meets an old mute (Max Von Sydow, who received an Oscar nomination for his role), as well as a woman with a troubled marriage (Viola Davis).

The film is certainly well-made, with plenty of outstanding performances, and a few key scenes that ring true. The actor who comes off the best is von Sydow, whose commanding voice is ironically absent here, but whose immense acting talent comes through, particularly with a heart-wrenching scene toward the end where Oskar plays him his dad's final answering machine messages. Horn is solid in the lead role, if a bit overwrought at times, and Davis does wonders with an underwritten part. The major climactic scene with Horn and Jeffrey Wright is also handled well.

Unfortunately, for every scene that works, three scenes don't. The biggest problem with the movie, of course, is that the horrors of 9/11 are still so raw, and so real, that a fictionalized account of that day, about characters who weren't really there, just feels wrong. Why should we care about fictional characters responding to the attacks, when we're already so aware of the true life heroes and victims and sacrifices from that day? *United 93* is one of the great films of the mid-2000s, but that movie puts us into a situation that really happened, to uncompromising visceral effect. *Extremely Loud & Incredibly Close* isn't as effective because we're supposed to identify with flat fictional characters who aren't developed enough to earn our sympathy. Of course a fictionalized account of a true life disaster can work—*Titanic* being one of the best examples—but 9/11 is still so recent that there better be a good reason for it. And this movie just isn't it.

It's not just the 9/11 aspect that brings the film down. Even if it were about a fictional traumatic event, it wouldn't work. Director Daldry has had great success working with kids (*Billy Elliot*) and making searing dramas (*The Hours*), but *Extremely Loud & Incredibly Close* is the first film he's made that misses the mark. His directorial flourishes are way overdone, and the sentimentality bar is always raised three notches too high. The film never finds the right pacing, with too much of it feeling episodic; some scenes go on forever, and others are way too short. The most glaring error the film makes is never making the father seem like a real, warm-blooded person. We only see him in flashbacks, mostly viewed from Oskar's point of view, and he's perceived as so perfect that he never becomes three-dimensional. His games with his son are adorable, and his voice messages are haunting, but the role never becomes anything more than just Tom Hanks playing a dad.

And then there's Sandra. Did she make a mistake following up *The Blind Side* with this film? Absolutely not. While the film *is* disappointing (don't let that inexplicable

Oscar nomination for Best Picture fool you), she comes off rather well, for the most part. She was wise in taking a supporting role, giving her a little quiet time in the four years that separated *The Proposal* and *The Blind Side* from *The Heat* and *Gravity*. She only has about twenty minutes of screen-time in the film's 130-minute running time, but she makes the most of them, with a harrowing two-scenes-in-a-row punch about halfway through. While Hanks is never given any significant lengthy scene, we get to know Sandra's character of Linda a lot more, as she comes to deal with the death of her husband. Since the film is told from Oskar's point of view, we see Linda in the first half as a distant figure, someone who just knocks on the door occasionally and asks if he's okay. He had much more of a connection with his dad, so he's not happy that he's now stuck day to day with his dour mom. Not all of Sandra's moments here work, with one too many scenes of her shoving her hand against her mouth and crying, and one particularly baffling scene that opens with a shot of Sandra just standing in a room and oddly staring past the camera.

No, Sandra shines in two scenes halfway through that finally bring her character to life. Oskar wakes her up in the middle of the night and starts talking her ear off, asking her questions, making her finally explode at him in the kitchen. Sandra is mesmerizing in this scene, in her rage, in her mix of emotions. Linda doesn't want to yell at her son, but he keeps feeding her anger until she can't hold it in anymore. Probably the most shocking element to this scene, is the ending, when Oskar tells her, "I wish it were you in the building instead of him." Instead of blowing up at him again, she says, solemnly, "So do I." This moment is heartbreaking, and comes off totally natural, unlike so much else in the movie.

After this, we flash to the morning of the "Worst Day," as Oskar calls it, when her husband calls her to tell him he's in the tower, and that he's going to be okay. Her trembling fear as she walks to the window and begs him to stay on the phone with her is unnervingly real. Even though the scene is strange in that it's one of the few in the film that *isn't* from Oskar's perspective, it gives us more insight into Linda, and the horror in the waiting she endured that day. The film might have been improved with a few more scenes like this, away from Oskar. Sandra actually shot a couple of scenes with the late James Gandolfini, who played a 9/11 widow and potential love interest. Test audiences apparently rejected these scenes, prompting Daldry to leave the material on the cutting room floor. These scenes did not appear on the DVD, and, especially with Gandolfini's sudden passing, I'd love to see them pop up on a future DVD release someday. A little more development of her character in the middle portion of the film would have been ideal.

Sandra mostly disappears after the phone call flashback, until her final major sequence at the end of the film that finally explains her journey. A question that nags at you the whole time while watching the movie is, why does Linda allow her son to just roam around the city without her close supervision? He's nine years old, for God's sake! In the end we discover that she's been keeping up with him the whole time, always one step ahead and keeping track of his whereabouts. The two actors are so warm and tender in this scene, with Sandra so heartfelt when she says, "I miss his voice telling me he loves me." The film lacked these authentic quieter moments, the kinds of scenes that allow the viewer to spend quality time with the characters. So much of the movie requires the viewer to keep up with the breathless Oskar, and not enough time to allow for the supporting characters to make enough of an impression. Sandra's final scene is simple and moving, when she finds Oskar's book and takes in the various pages, with her reactions doing all the work. Until *Gravity*, Sandra so rarely just reacted on screen, with no trite dialogue to follow, that I found this, maybe more than any other, to be her most refreshing moment in the movie.

Sandra is by no means extraordinary in *Extremely Loud & Incredibly Close*—it's a solid, unmemorable performance that doesn't reach the heights of her startling work in *Infamous*, *The Blind Side*, or, of course, *Gravity*—but she gets the opportunity to stretch her dramatic muscles and show that she's up to the task of exploring more wounded, downbeat characters. She's an A-list star who could have done anything after winning the Oscar, and she chose a supporting role in a film that gave her the chance to work with Daldry, Hanks, and a talented child actor making his film debut. While the movie didn't net her any awards, it gave audiences a preview of what was to come at the end of 2013.

Yes, Alfonso Cuaron's *Gravity* was almost here.

BEST SCENE

Sandra explodes at her son in the kitchen.

BEST LINE

"It's not gonna make sense, because it doesn't!"

FUN FACTS

Sandra was in New York with her family at the time of the September 11 attacks and had a clear view of the towers.

Sandra's lone acting nomination for this film was Best Supporting Actress at the Georgia Film Critics Association.

Sandra and Hanks were voted number one and two trustworthy celebrities in the Reader's Digest poll in 2013.

Von Sydow turned down the role of Hal in *Beginners*, which later went to Christopher Plummer, in favor of playing the mute in this film. Both men were nominated for Best Supporting Actor, and Plummer won.

Viola Davis appeared in two films in 2011 that were nominated for a Best Picture Oscar. The second was *The Help*, which also earned her a Best Actress nomination.

Horn came to the attention of Daldry when he won on a Kid's Week episode of *Jeopardy!*

To date, Sandra has appeared in four films that have gone on to be nominated for Best Picture at the Academy Awards.

This is the first film Daldry directed that didn't earn him an Oscar nomination. He was nominated for all three of his prior films—*Billy Elliot*, *The Hours*, and *The Reader*.

THE HEAT
(2013)

FILM FACTS

DISTRIBUTOR: 20th Century Fox
PRODUCTION COMPANY: Chernin Entertainment
RELEASE DATE: June 28, 2013

DIRECTOR: Paul Feig
WRITER: Katie Dippold
PRODUCERS: Peter Chernin, Jenno Topping
ALSO STARRING: Melissa McCarthy, Demian Bichir, Marlon
Wayans, Thomas F. Wilson, Jane Curtain

REVIEW

After Sandra started winning awards for dramatic work,
some might have assumed she would say good-bye to
comedy for good. But Sandra ultimately did what she does
best—surprise us. She's one of the best in the business
because she's able to effortlessly bounce back and forth
between genres, and now that some rich opportunities have
come her way, 2013 arrived with not one but two hugely
anticipated Sandra movies. And they couldn't be any
different from each other. Who but Sandra follows a
raucous R-rated buddy comedy with a quiet two-person
thriller set in space? 2009, with the varied trio of *The*

Proposal, *All About Steve*, and *The Blind Side*, looked to be her most epic year ever.

Then along came 2013.

Following her Oscar win for *The Blind Side*, Sandra shot *Extremely Loud & Incredibly Close* and *Gravity* back to back, two films that screamed class and innovation, and it looked like she might, at least for awhile, move away from the comedy genre. While *The Proposal* was a smash, *All About Steve* was a disaster, and if Sandra was going to return to the kinds of films most of her casual fans love her in, she was going to have to choose carefully. In the end, she couldn't have picked a better project than *The Heat*. While this isn't one of her most memorable movies, the film offers two hours of glorious entertainment simply in watching two gifted comedic actresses share the screen together. And best of all, this film gave Sandra the opportunity to say something in a comedy she hadn't said since *Two if by Sea*, nearly twenty years prior. She gets to say fuck. A lot.

The Heat was a wise choice for Sandra to make because it would have been startling for this movie not to work. Sandra is just naturally funny, so pairing her up with the hilarious and talented Melissa McCarthy was a masterstroke. McCarthy first made an impression on me when she played Sookie on *Gilmore Girls*, and for so many years, she was always just Lorelai's best friend in Stars Hollow. Then, along came *Bridesmaids*, the funniest movie of 2011. And in an ensemble of great actresses, McCarthy became the standout, earning a rare Academy Award nomination for a comedic performance. McCarthy and that film's director, Paul Feig, wanted to work on another project again—who better than Sandra to join the party? Sandra has seemed lost in some of her recent comedies, like *Miss Congeniality 2* and *All About Steve*. But she's in top form here, with a natural chemistry with McCarthy that makes for a real crowd-pleaser.

Sandra plays Sarah Ashburn, a Special Agent who cares to focus more on her career than her personal life, and who doesn't always blend well with all the other FBI operatives in the field. When she's up for a promotion, she's forced to go to Boston to solve a case and prove her worth. But little does she know that a very different kind of interrogator— ruthless, potty-mouthed detective Mullins (McCarthy)—is about to become her full-time partner, as they try to take down an invisible drug lord. They're combative at first, but as their inner demons come out, they start to realize they're more alike than they realized, and what started as contentiousness, soon becomes a budding friendship.

One element about this role I noticed immediately was the similarities it shares to other characters Sandra has played in past films, many of which have been comedies. A woman who's forever single, and dedicated only to her job? Think Lucy in *While You Were Sleeping* (token taker), or Angela in *The Net* (computer programmer), or Margaret in *The Proposal* (book editor). And then there's Grace in *Miss Congeniality*, the FBI agent who had to become a beauty contestant to take down the bad guy. When I first saw the trailer of *The Heat* at the end of 2012, my heart dropped a little, because it looked like Sandra was just playing a variation on her *Miss Congeniality* character. FBI agent?

Check. Socially awkward? Check, check. Was this film just going to be *Miss Congeniality 3*?

Thankfully, Sandra gives this character her own unique spin. She's not a goofy slob like Grace, or a hopeless romantic like Lucy, or a ruthless career woman like Margaret. Special Agent Ashburn is good at what she does, but she doesn't relate well to others, and has to make an effort to fit in. We discover her family history, and how that has affected her life. We learn of her high school yearbook, which was greeted with only two signatures, both by teachers, one saying, "Good luck, student," and the other saying, "It will get better." She has never been in a stable relationship, and has never been able to make a true friend. Enter the life force that is Mullens. Different from Ashburn in every way, Mullens is still instantly drawn to the less confident Ashburn, and the two become a team to be reckoned with.

Looking over Sandra's career, it's surprising to note that she had never made a major R-rated comedy before. There's the little seen *When the Party's Over* from 1993, and her first big dud post-*Speed*, 1996's *Two if by Sea*, but over the last twenty years, she has stuck mostly to PG-13-rated entertainments. I'm sure this has never been a conscious effort on her part—maybe a smart R-rated comedy script had simply never come across her desk—but one of the joys of *The Heat* is in watching McCarthy, and Sandra toward the end, drop one F-bomb after another. One review pointed out how much more interesting the movie might have been if Sandra and McCarthy had *switched* roles, and I'd be lying if I didn't think the same thing. It might not have worked, but wouldn't it have been fun to see them try? As Ashburn, Sandra doesn't start talking like McCarthy until the finale, when she lets loose—to hilarious results. One of the movie's most memorable scenes has her calling a bunch of cops jerks, then shit jerks, then... well... you'll just have to see the film to find out.

It has been noted as being a rare female buddy cop movie, but what I found even more remarkable about *The Heat* was that it shows two strong women on-screen who are one-hundred-percent committed to their jobs, the kind that men typically occupy. Hollywood studio execs are always surprised every few months when a movie starring women opens well and, even better, has staying power at the box office (*Bridesmaids*, for example, opened with $26 million but stuck around long enough to make $167 million domestically). Opening *The Heat* at the end of June, in a summer of bloated, male-driven action movies, was a brilliant release strategy; more women are seeing movies at this time of year than men, and they want to see strong, capable women on-screen, especially those whose lives don't revolve around relationships with men. *The Heat* isn't a great film, but it's further proof that audiences are hungry for funny female-driven pictures.

So how is *The Heat*, just as a movie, especially in a summer so bereft of good comedies? It's one of those films that get the job done, that leaves you walking out of the theater smiling. It does have a few very big laughs, and the chemistry between the two leads is fantastic. It's entertaining throughout, and it slips in a cute underlying message about friendship, especially with a closing scene, involving the aforementioned yearbook, that works way better than it deserves to. The sequence where they get drunk is a standout, and a moment toward the end, when something sharp finds itself in Sarah's leg, is hilarious. Ultimately, though, the film will not be remembered as one of Sandra's best comedies, for one simple reason: the plot of the movie, involving the investigation of the Boston drug lord, is sloppy and uninvolving. The lame plot of *The Heat* is basically an excuse to team up these two gifted comediennes, and all of the scenes that involve them playing off each other work great; it's when the stupid story keeps rearing its ugly head that the movie goes off the rails a little, especially with its unbelievable reveal of the villain, and the way each bad guy in the last half-hour keeps talking when in reality he would just be shooting the two women dead. While the movie is fun, and the performances of both stars are terrific, a really great story would have made this a modern comedy classic.

The Heat falls somewhere in the middle of Sandra's comedies, with *While You Were Sleeping* remaining the all-time champ, and *All About Steve* forever rotting in the sewers of movie hell. I'd put it one notch below *Miss Congeniality* and *The Proposal*, but one notch above *Two Weeks Notice*, and plenty of notches above *Practical Magic*, *Forces of Nature*, and *Miss Congeniality 2*. It will be interesting to revisit *The Heat* in a few years to see how it holds up. And who knows? With a $40 million opening weekend, and a final gross that equaled the box office total of *The Proposal*, it's possible *The Heat 2* could be in our futures. But as Sandra said in an Extra interview in the summer of 2013, "My sequels have never done well," so I'd imagine it would take an awesome script to bring the two back. If nothing else, it would be pretty easy to top *Miss Congeniality 2* and *Speed 2*. If they ever were to make a second one, I would suggest they put more effort in the central investigation of the storyline, give it a little more weight and meaning. These are two of our brightest, most interesting actresses working today, and they deserve only the best.

As we move into the future, past *Gravity* and beyond, it's a relief to note that Sandra, who could have stayed the route of many Academy Award winners and churned out stupid blockbusters and pretentious dramatic drivel, has chosen to take chances with ambitious projects, and have a little fun with boozy, outrageous comedies like *The Heat*. She may be referred to as Oscar winner Sandra Bullock from here on out, but she's not afraid to go back to what we all know and love her in—the comedy genre. Here's hoping Sandra keeps doing what she's doing, jetting back and forth between the prestige and the puerile, and having loads of fun in the process.

BEST SCENE
After avoiding a potty mouth seemingly her entire life, Sandra finally lashes out at the Boston cops.

BEST LINE
"You just gave me a ring, MOTHERFUCKER!"

FUN FACTS

Ashburn's yearbook is Sandra's actual 1982 yearbook from Washington-Lee High School in Arlington, Virginia. The art department digitally manipulated Sandra's real class photo to include glasses and braces.

Sandra's third film as an FBI Agent, following the two *Miss Congeniality* movies.

Director Feig plays the hospital doctor who complains about the excessive profanity.

The man McCarthy kisses in the bar is her real life husband and *Bridesmaids* co-star Ben Falcone.

Sandra won Choice Summer Movie Star: Female and Choice Movie Chemistry at the Teen Choice Awards. The film also won Favorite Comedic Movie at the People's Choice Awards.

GRAVITY
(2013)

FILM FACTS

DISTRIBUTOR: Warner Bros.
PRODUCTION COMPANY: Heyday Films
RELEASE DATE: October 4, 2013

DIRECTOR: Alfonso Cuaron
WRITERS: Alfonso Cuaron, Jonas Cuaron
PRODUCERS: Alfonso Cuaron, David Heyman
ALSO STARRING: George Clooney

REVIEW

Fans of Sandra have been waiting twenty years for *Gravity*. Ever since she broke through in 1994 with her charismatic performance in the action extravaganza *Speed*, she has been working steadily in films, both good and bad. From 1995 to 2008 she had a string of hits—*While You Were Sleeping*, *A Time to Kill*, *Miss Congeniality*—as well as a boatload of bombs—*Two if By Sea*, *Forces of Nature*, *Gun Shy*. She has been a beloved actress among film fans for two decades, but after the critical and financial failure of her suspense thriller *Premonition* in 2007, it seemed like she would never break through her long-lasting trend of making mediocre films. But two films in 2009 changed everything. While she did appear that year in *All About Steve*, arguably her worst film ever, she also starred in *The Proposal* and *The Blind Side*, two smash hits that re-instated her A-list status and garnered her not just monetary success but critical cred and major awards, including the Golden Globe Award, Screen Actors Guild Award, and Academy Award for *The Blind Side*.

After Sandra enjoyed such a spectacular year, one might assume there was nowhere left for her to go but down. The next three years offered little output from her, with only a brief turn in *Extremely Loud & Incredibly Close* and the occasional film premiere appearance. However, 2013 marked something impressive for Sandra: her most astonishing year yet, both financially and critically. Think her PG-13-rated romantic comedy *The Proposal* earning $163 million nationwide was a fluke? Consider her 2013 summer comedy *The Heat*, co-starring Melissa McCarthy, which earned $159 million—with an R rating, which precludes most teenagers and kids from buying tickets. Think *The Blind Side* making $256 million nationwide was impossible for Sandra to ever beat? That film made headlines in early 2010 for making the most money in history with only a sole female name above the poster.

Still, remarkably, her newest film *Gravity* beat her all-time record. Opening with an astonishing $55 million, the largest sum a film has ever made on a weekend in October, *Gravity* went on in the next two months to become one of the biggest smash hits of the year, topping out at $273 million nationwide and a whopping $714 million worldwide. Many expect a summer action movie like *The Avengers* and *Iron Man 3* to break box office records, but few assumed *Gravity*, with its fall release date and quieter marketing campaign, would reach such similar heights in its popularity. The film is, after all, a drama more than it is a thriller, one that features only one person on screen for the majority of its running time. *Gravity* is a deeply intimate, emotionally rewarding film experience, and the rare instance of a great motion picture that has managed to appeal to everyone—film buffs, casual moviegoers, grandparents, kids. It has visionary special effects, a fun supporting turn by George Clooney, and a moving story that creeps up on the viewer as the film reaches its stunning climax. Best of all, it features a stunning performance by Sandra that bests anything she has ever done on screen, including *Crash*, *Infamous*, and *The Blind Side*.

Gravity was in the works for more than five years. Alfonso Cuaron, one of the most acclaimed filmmakers of his generation, wanted to make a movie set in space. The director of such terrific and diverse films as *A Little Princess*, *Harry Potter and the Prisoner of Azkaban*, and *Y Tu Mama Tambien* wanted to step outside his comfort zone and do something different. While his 2006 film *Children of Men* was not a major moneymaker, its overwhelming critical praise and handful of Academy Award nominations gave him enough clout to begin the process on his next motion picture. Cuaron has said that *Gravity* was the biggest miscalculation of his entire career, in that he had no idea how long it would take to get his vision to the screen. When he approached his longtime cinematographer

Emmanuel Lubezki about this project, Cuaron said that the process could be completed relatively quickly—a year, he assumed—considering that it was essentially a two-character piece with little dialogue. *Gravity*, however, took much longer, both to get off the ground and to become realized, with a considerable amount of time devoted to figuring out how the screenplay could be translated to the screen. Cuaron met with major filmmakers who had worked on complicated special effects films before, like James Cameron, the maverick director of *Avatar*, who told Cuaron flat out that the technology to make *Gravity* was at least five more years away. Cuaron and his crew wouldn't take no for answer, though, and after much research and determination, they ended up inventing brand new technology just to get the film made.

As the team behind *Gravity* started experimenting with these mind-blowing technologies, Cuaron met with potential actors. Angelina Jolie was the first to be cast as Dr. Ryan Stone, but she dropped out due to scheduling conflicts, and Cuaron went on to consider Natalie Portman, Marion Cotillard, and Scarlett Johansson. The one who proved to be the best choice for the role, as it turned out, was Sandra, and he approached her at her home in Texas, during the summer of 2010. She was hesitant to take the role at first, having endured a very public break-up with her former husband Jesse James, and taking care of a newly adopted child Louis at home. Sandra was in awe of Cuaron's work, however, and had been hoping for an opportunity to work with him. She eventually signed on, making *Gravity* one of her first two projects following her

Oscar win for *The Blind Side*. Early in pre-production, Robert Downey Jr. was attached to the role of Matt Kowalski, the only other major character in the film, but he eventually dropped out, too, for undisclosed reasons, and George Clooney came on board the project, marking the first time that Sandra and Clooney—close friends since they were struggling actors in the late 1980s—finally worked together in a movie.

Soon after Sandra wrapped her small part in *Extremely Loud & Incredibly Close*, she flew to London and began work prepping for *Gravity*. To achieve all that was needed of her on this unusual production, Sandra spent months training with two fitness instructors who specifically aimed to strengthen her core. During the production, she spent long hours hanging on wires, and she needed to be in tremendous shape to physically endure the trying and claustrophobic shoot. It was the most demanding filming experience of her career, with Sandra at times having to spend up to ten hours a day stuck inside a tiny nine-by-nine light box on a bare soundstage all alone, acting off nobody, and having little human interaction. Clooney was on set for only a small part of the shoot, and before and after his scenes were filmed, the *Gravity* production was essentially a one-woman show.

After Sandra wrapped her work on the film, she went on to star in *The Heat* with Melissa McCarthy, while the technical wizards behind *Gravity* spent more than two years in post bringing Cuaron's vision to life. It was one of those hot projects everyone in Hollywood knew about, but who few knew of any concrete details. The first release date set for the film was November 2012, but *Gravity* was ultimately delayed due to the extensive post-production work that needed to be completed, and the film was ultimately pushed back to October 4, 2013. *Gravity* finally had its world premiere at the Venice Film Festival at the end of August, and instantly received unanimous praise from critics, with many calling the film a landmark in cinema, as well as a tremendous showcase for its main star. While it may have taken Cuaron multiple years to get the film made, his hard work paid off, with audiences all over the world falling in love with this remarkable achievement.

There have been spectacular opening shots in films over the years—the first few minutes of Orson Welles' *Touch of Evil* come to mind—but the thirteen-minute shot that kicks *Gravity* into high gear might be the most astonishing of all time. The film opens simply, cutting to a quiet and awe-inspiring shot of planet Earth. There is no music, no dialogue. Director Cuaron draws the viewer into the movie slowly, allowing him time to situate himself in a setting very few people are familiar with. Clooney's voice is soon heard, and when he and Sandra finally appear on-screen, one is completely immersed in the amazing oasis of outer space. The actors talk for a few minutes—telling jokes, voicing frustrations, uttering the briefest accounts of their lives—and the viewer watches in awe as the camera spins around the characters and gives alternating angles of people floating hundreds of miles above Earth. But then, the unthinkable happens—debris from a destroyed Russian satellite zooms straight toward the space shuttle and collides with such ferocity that Ryan gets ejected from her spot and starts flipping into the void of space. All of these events play out in real time, in one unbroken shot, a seamless piece of pure cinema that is a work of art all its own.

Once the first harrowing action scene reaches its climax, the rest of the film plays out as an intense survival story, with Ryan doing all she can to return to Earth. The second half of the movie finds Ryan working all by her lonesome, overcoming one potentially fatal obstacle after another, in order to survive. Cuaron has said that one of his influences in making *Gravity* was the first major work by Steven Spielberg—*Duel*, the 1971 TV movie about an ordinary man who is pursued by a mad trucker. Spielberg's film doesn't let up in the suspense and tension throughout its brief ninety-minute running time, and neither does *Gravity*. The scene of Ryan and Matt trying to grab onto the shuttle, for instance, offers no break from the kind of hold-your-breath excitement that one rarely experiences in modern movies, and a later scene involving a second run-in with the satellite debris is so well realized that it is hard to not have a strong physical reaction to what is playing out on the screen.

How *Gravity* differs from so many other action films set in space is that it has a heartbreaking, intimate story at its core, one that slowly but assuredly works its power over the viewer. There is not a lot of backstory in *Gravity*. The viewer is introduced at the beginning to two characters who he comes to know little about, until about thirty minutes in, when he learns that one reason Ryan accepted the mission into space is that she has endured an unthinkable loss in her life. She tells Matt that she had a daughter, a precious little girl with brown hair who died in a tragic accident at her elementary school. One would argue that there is nothing worse for a parent than to bury his or her own child, and Ryan has dealt with her own pain by removing herself from the world—literally. When she's suddenly the last survivor of her mission, and has to go to extreme lengths to stay alive, she is faced with the ultimate question: why go on living when there's nothing left to live for?

At one point in the movie, Ryan hits a stumbling block, when her shuttle shuts down and loses all its fuel. She immediately gives up, turns down the oxygen, and prepares herself for death. Up until this point, the film has worked as an exciting suspense thriller, with enough beauty in its impeccable visuals to guarantee unanimous praise. It is in this long, quiet scene, however, that *Gravity* moves into truly special territory. The camera lingers on Ryan's face, as she starts to cry, realizing she is moments away from fading, never to come back. It is a raw, intimate moment rarely seen in a modern American blockbuster. Most directors would cut away, move to the next scene, do his best to not make the audience feel even remotely uncomfortable. Cuaron is gutsier than the average director, however, because he understands that the viewer has spent an hour with this character, rooting her on, and hoping she makes it back to Earth. The viewer is so invested in her plight that he wants to share this downbeat moment with her, still with the hope that she will persevere and not give up so easily.

214

Ryan's determination to stay alive brings the film to a moving and satisfying conclusion. Cuaron doesn't allow for much sentimentality in the movie, but he does give Ryan a tender monologue, where she talks to the invisible Matt about when he will meet her little girl. This scene, more than any other in the film, had the possibility of playing maudlin, but Sandra underplays it, not going overboard with the tears or any look-at-me kind of emotion. All it takes is one brief hesitation at the end of the monologue, when she looks up at the shuttle ceiling and takes a deep breath, to tell everything the viewer needs to know about her state of mind. As she hurtles in a small burning pod toward Earth, not knowing if she has a chance to survive, she screams in terrified delight that whether she burns up in the next few minutes or makes it to safety, it has been one hell of a ride. The last shot of the movie, another long take that is a perfect bookend to the first shot of the film, shows Ryan swim to the shore and try, with humorous difficulty, to stand up, and finally surrender herself to—what else—gravity.

In a recent interview, James Cameron said how much he loved *Gravity*, that he thought it was the best space film ever made. Cameron would know—as the director of *Aliens* and *Avatar*, he has been to space before. Movies set in space are relatively few and far between, with only two to three significant films in this science fiction subgenre released each year. The first space motion picture ever made was *A Trip to the Moon*, directed by George Melies and released in 1902, and over the decades many influential films followed, like *The Day the Earth Stood Still*, *Star Wars*,

Alien, and *Contact.* More recent examples of this subgenre of science fiction films include the latest *Star Trek* films, as well as Ridley Scott's *Prometheus.* So many of these films, however, don't take outer space seriously, and instead treat it like a fantasy world, with monsters and aliens forever running amok. The space film closest in tone and grandeur to *Gravity* is Stanley Kubrick's 1968 masterpiece, *2001: A Space Odyssey,* which is dead serious in tone, and more interested in making audiences think than it is in blowing up a distant planet. The film offered audiences not only some of the most stunning visual effects ever seen on screen up to that point, but also the first truly awesome look at space, and not until *Gravity* had moviegoers been treated to a spectacle that can match it.

One of the most impressive achievements of *Gravity* is its focus on a female main character for the majority of its running time. Cuaron was pressured by Warner Bros. to make the main character a man, as many studio executives still think to this day that audiences won't go to a big blockbuster movie if a woman is leading the show. Cuaron, to his credit, never wavered from his vision, and stuck to his guns about hiring an actress for the pivotal central role of Dr. Ryan Stone. While it is not common for women to headline big-budget action thrillers, a few select actresses have paved the way for Sandra's role in *Gravity.* The most obvious influence is Sigourney Weaver, Sandra's *Infamous* co-star, who made huge strides for women in action cinema when she outlived all the men and became the heroine of 1979's *Alien.* A riveting space film in its own right, as quiet in its many suspenseful moments the same way *Gravity* is,

Alien offered Weaver the chance to prove that women can hold their own in big-budgeted movies the same way that men can. Her character of Ellen Ripley is witty and intelligent, and quick thinking in the face of adversity, just like Dr. Ryan Stone is in *Gravity*. Weaver followed her tremendous work in that Ridley Scott classic by reprising the role in three sequels, but despite the occasional action movie female lead—Geena Davis headlined 1996's *The Long Kiss Goodnight*, and faced scrutiny when the film bombed hard at the box office—men typically drive the genre. For a major studio film like *Gravity* to feature not just a female in the lead role but a woman in her late forties, particularly in today's teen-driven marketplace, is an important step in the right direction; hopefully the film's massive box office success should point studio executives to offering roles like this to more women in the future.

Alfonso Cuaron has been working his whole impressive career toward *Gravity*, and with his latest film he has catapulted himself into the realm of the top three filmmakers working in the medium today. He started quietly in the 1990s, helming film versions of two classic novels, *A Little Princess* and *Great Expectations*. He impressed audiences with his low-budget Spanish road trip movie, *Y Tu Mama Tambien*, and stumped many when he was chosen over many A-listers to helm the third *Harry Potter* movie, *Harry Potter and the Prisoner of Azkaban*. While the darker, more immersive vision he brought to the franchise won him fans, it was his phenomenal work on his 2006 dystopian drama *Children of Men* that cemented his status as a true auteur. The story of a future society where women can no longer bare children, *Children of Men* introduced his famous long takes, and catapulted Cuaron to legendary status.

Gravity, remarkably, is an even greater achievement, the kind of film so few directors would have had the patience, or the determination, or the imagination, to ever make. He succeeded in creating a film that is unlike anything that's come before; while movies have taken us to space time and time again throughout the medium's history, nothing has ever demonstrated the true beauty of space quite like *Gravity*. He also succeeded in telling a moving, intimate story about a woman in her forties who has lost everything, and who finds the will to live even in the most trying of circumstances. The film works as a tense thriller, an emotional drama, an action blockbuster, and a bravura one-woman survival tale. That Cuaron worked on it tirelessly, day and night, for nearly five years, also shows the determination he has to get his films as perfect as possible. The film is a piece of pure artistic genius, and while Sandra and the cinematographer Emmanuel Lubezki also deserve kudos for their fantastic work, *Gravity* begins and ends with the great Alfonso Cuaron.

Aside from some voice-work at the beginning of the film by Ed Harris, the star of two famous space films *The Right Stuff* and *Apollo 13*, *Gravity* features only two performances, and while the film belongs to Sandra, Clooney is equally impressive in his brief but essential role. Matt is a jokester, giving the film its only sources of comic relief when he tells humorous stories from his past, right before the first wave of satellite debris hits the station. With so much action and intensity throughout, *Gravity* might have been too much of a downer without at least some comedy woven into the narrative, and Clooney provides just the right number of laughs in a few key moments to give the audience a much needed relief from the tension. His humor also adds to the emotion of the movie, because after so much of his commentary lightens up what is otherwise a scary circumstance, he turns serious in a moment of self-sacrifice. If the character hadn't been so personable before, this scene of *Gravity* might not have had the power that it does. His sweet, self-mocking personality makes the awesome spectacle more easily accessible in the beginning, and his chemistry with Sandra is natural throughout the brief running time they share together. The role of Matt is pivotal to the success of the movie, and no one could have inhabited this role better than Clooney.

Sandra, however, is the star, and she is a revelation in *Gravity*. America's sweetheart for so many years, the lead actress in so many terrific comedies and dramas over the last two decades, she is loved the world over—and still, nobody could have been prepared for her mesmerizing, physically demanding, emotionally rich tour-de-force of a performance she delivers in this film. So much of *Gravity* depends on visual effects, and another actress could have gotten lost somewhere behind all that beautiful imagery. Even when the viewer can only see her face inside a space suit for the first thirty minutes, her presence is felt in each second of screen time. The quiet despair she displays is evident from her first shot on screen, when she is focused on the technical job she has at hand. When the debris hits, she panics and screams, like any normal person would do, but when she makes it back to the shuttle and finds herself the sole survivor, Sandra's rarely utilized physicality comes into play. In the film's most striking shot of all, Ryan enters the shuttle, takes off her heavy suit, and curls up into a fetal position, in mid-air, signifying a moment of rebirth. From this point on, no one is helping her, and she needs to fend for herself, like a newborn child. What follows are many scenes of physical tasks and problems to solve, as she slowly realizes she might not survive the strenuous ordeal. The up-and-down emotions her character goes through would be a lot for an actress to deal with in a film that takes place down on Earth, let alone in zero gravity, and Sandra is more than up to the task. She has to not only convey everything her character is thinking and feeling at all times, but also deal with the tremendously demanding physical side of the role. That such a moving performance broke through under these circumstances is some minor miracle. Later nominated for her second Best Actress Oscar at the 86th Annual Academy Awards, Sandra is the best she has ever been, in this, the film of her career.

Gravity is proof that studio filmmaking in the new millennium still has the capability to be strong and inventive, and promote the imagination. While the television medium has enjoyed a new golden age over the last ten years, some have argued that major motion pictures have been declining in quality, especially studio blockbusters, which are often dumbed down, and aimed at kids and teenagers, to make the highest profit possible. *Gravity*, however, stands out as a true anomaly; it is a big-budget studio film made with love and artistry, that was geared toward an adult audience, that allows for a woman in her late forties to command the screen all by herself, and that promotes ideas over explosions. *Gravity* is an astonishing film, an instant classic, and it offers fans of Sandra, after twenty long years, a reason to celebrate.

BEST SCENE
Sandra starts weeping when she realizes she's about to die.

BEST LINE
"Either way, it's going to be one hell of a ride."

FUN FACTS

Gravity won seven Academy Awards, including Best Director, Best Cinematography, and Best Editing. It lost Best Picture to *12 Years a Slave*, and Sandra lost Best Actress to Cate Blanchett, for *Blue Jasmine*.

Aningaaq, the man Sandra talks to over the shortwave radio, is the main character of the companion short film *Aningaaq*, directed by Jonas Cuaron, which shows the other side of the conversation.

For research, Sandra talked to Astronaut Cady Coleman about life in space.

Because of Cuaron's lengthy takes, Sandra had to memorize long combinations of precise movements to hit her marks at different points in the shot, as well as coordinate her own moves with those of the wire rig attached to her and the camera.

Along with *12 Years a Slave*, *Gravity* is the first film in history to tie for Best Picture at the Producers Guild Awards.

While filming the underwater scene, Cuaron held his breath along with Sandra to make sure he wasn't asking too much of his leading lady. He soon found that he couldn't match her lung power.

The film was shot on digital cameras. However, the last scene of the movie was filmed in sixty-five millimeter, in order to give a hyper-reality look.

With more than forty feature films behind her, *Gravity* is Sandra's most successful motion picture to date.

CONCLUSION

Sandra Bullock has been on one hell of a ride—and she's enjoyed one hell of a career. When in the early 2000s it looked like she would languish in romantic comedy hell forever, she finally broke through in films like *Crash*, *Infamous*, and *The Blind Side* to become an actress who is finally being taken seriously. While *Speed* remained her best movie for nearly two decades, that terrific action film was finally eclipsed by Alfonso Cuaron's masterpiece, *Gravity*. When many doubted she would ever be considered for a major award nomination, she was nominated and won the Oscar for *The Blind Side*, and then was nominated again just four years later for *Gravity*. Sandra Bullock is a worldwide treasure. And as she continues on, starring in hopefully many more films to come, expect me to be there, rooting her on, every step of the way.

ABOUT THE AUTHOR

Brian Rowe graduated from Loyola Marymount University, where he studied English & Film. He has written ten novels and dozens of short stories. He is currently pursuing his MA in English-Writing at the University of Nevada, Reno, and is hard at work on his next novel.

The Sandra Bullock Files: From Speed to Gravity is Brian's first non-fiction book.

ALSO BY BRIAN ROWE

Slate
Townhouse
Happy Birthday to Me
Happy Birthday to Me Again
Happy Birthday to You
The Vampire Underground
The Zombie Playground
The Monster Apocalypse
Over the Rainbow

CONNECT WITH BRIAN ONLINE

Brian's Web Site
http://brianrowebooks.com

———

6362945R00128

Printed in Great Britain
by Amazon.co.uk, Ltd.,
Marston Gate.